Y0-CUX-922

BY CLAYTON ESHLEMAN:

Mexico & North (1961)
Residence on Earth (translations of Pablo Neruda) (1962)
The Chavin Illumination (1965)
State of the Union (translations of Aimé Césaire, with Denis Kelly) (1966)
Lachrymae Mateo (1966)
Walks (1967)
Poemas Humanos/Human Poems (translations of César Vallejo) (1968)
Brother Stones (with William Paden's woodcuts) (1968)
Cantaloups & Splendor (1968)
T'ai (1969)
The House of Okumura (1969)
The House of Ibuki (1969)
Indiana (1969)
Yellow River Record (1969)
A Pitchblende (1969)
Bearings (1971)
Altars (1971)
A Caterpillar Anthology (editor & contributor) (1971)
The Sanjo Bridge (1972)
Coils (1973)
Human Wedding (1973)
Aux Morts (1974)
Spain, Take this Cup from Me (translations of Vallejo, with José Rubia Barcia) (1974)
Letter to André Breton (translation of Antonin Artaud) (1974)
Realignment (with drawings by Nora Jaffe) (1974)
Portrait of Francis Bacon (1975)
To Have Done with the Judgment of God (translation of Artaud, with Norman Glass) (1975)
The Gull Wall (1975)
Cogollo (1976)
Artaud the Mômo (translation of Artaud, with Norman Glass) (1976)
The Woman Who Saw through Paradise (1976)
Grotesca (1977)
On Mules Sent from Chavin (1977)
Core Meander (1977)
The Gospel of Celine Arnauld (1977)
Battles in Spain (translations of Vallejo, with José Rubia Barcia) (1978)
The Name Encanyoned River (1978)
What She Means (1978)
César Vallejo: The Complete Posthumous Poetry (with José Rubia Barcia) (1978)
A Note on Apprenticeship (1979)
The Lich Gate (1980)
Nights We Put the Rock Together (1980)
Our Lady of the Three-Pronged Devil (1980)
Hades in Manganese (1981)

Clayton Eshleman

HADES IN MANGANESE

Santa Barbara
BLACK SPARROW PRESS
1981

ACKNOWLEDGEMENTS

Some of these poems have appeared in *Atropos, Bachy, Cedar Rock, Difficulties, LA Weekly, Montemora, New Wilderness Letter, Other Islands, Partisan Review, Pequod, Poetry/LA, River Styx, Roadwork, Seneca Review* and *Text*. "Frida Kahlo's Release" appeared in *Out of the West* (Lord John Press, Northridge, California, 1979). A number of the poems also appeared in the following limited editions: *The Lich Gate* (Station Hill Press, Barrytown, New York, 1980), *Nights We Put the Rock Together* (Cadmus Editions, Santa Barbara, California, 1980), and *Our Lady of The Three-Pronged Devil* (Red Ozier Press, New York City, 1980). "Dot" was printed as a broadside by the Bellevue Press, Binghamton, New York, 1979. "The American Sublime" was printed as a post card by Station Hill Press, 1980. "For Aimé Césaire" shared a broadside with poems by Jerome Rothenberg and Diane Wakoski printed by Jazz Press, Los Angeles, 1980.

I would especially like to acknowledge the following: my wife Caryl who has helped me, at every stage, edit the 2000 pages of worksheets that went into this book; Robert Kelly, who made helpful editorial comments; and the Guggenheim Foundation for a Poetry Fellowship (1978/79) which enabled me to make a second visit to caves with paleolithic markings in southern France.

LIBRARY OF CONGRESS CATALOGING IN PUBLICATION DATA

Eshleman, Clayton.
  Hades in manganese.

  I. Title.
PS3555.S5H3   811'.54   80-20976
ISBN 0-87685-473-0
ISBN 0-87685-472-2 (pbk.)

A tentacle man dreaming in stone, of stone,
pregnant, falling line looped forward,
meandering out to

to—

to—

a dot. But on its other side his tentacle
remains detached, mirroring my fingertip,

my point,

sound trace and twin,

from Caryl

toward

Caryl

Table of Contents

PREFACE

I first visited the paleolithic painted caves when I spent four months near Les Eyzies, in the French Dordogne, in the spring/summer of 1974. I visited those caves that have been fixed up for tourists a dozen or so times, along with making one trip to Lascaux, the most famous cave in the area, which is officially closed.

When I returned to Los Angeles, I became aware that nearly all of the material on paleolithic caves treated the art as reflective of daytime activities, i.e., success in the hunt or fertility magic. The only person who impressed me as having looked at the signs and animals as possessing a coherence relative to themselves (in contrast to one *reflective* of hunting and eating activity) was André Leroi-Gourhan.[1] Unfortunately, what he drew from his experience, while original, seemed to be inadequate and based on juggled and incomplete data. Leroi-Gourhan argued that the animal juxtapositions represented sexual pairing, and that there was a predictable distribution of sexual pairs, animal types, and signs at the entrances, and in the corridors and recesses of the caves that he had either visited or studied. Reading this, I was puzzled, as my experience in a cave like Les Combarelles, for example, led me to think that the corridors there had been visited and engraved over thousands of years and that there was no plan to it whatsoever.

---

[1] There are some minor but interesting exceptions to this statement. Georges Bataille's Skira monograph on Lascaux, which draws on his book, *Eroticism*, is provocative if terribly Catholic. Charles Olson's lectures on "The New Science of Man," collected in *Olson #10*, are stimulating but, in contrast to his work on the Mayans, based entirely on the writing of others and hurriedly put together. Weston La Barre's chapter, "The Dancing Sorcerer," in his *The Ghost Dance*, while taking a traditional approach, is thrilling to read. The Ucko/Rosenthal *Paleolithic Cave Art* is the best introduction to the subject from a critique-survey viewpoint. The drawings by Abbés Breuil and Glory, based on engravings, are worth more than anything written, as a meditation on this art.

In 1978 my wife and I returned to the Dordogne. When we revisited Les Combarelles, I took Leroi-Gourhan's map and compared it with that of the Abbé Henri Breuil, in the possession of Claude Archambeau, the guide and caretaker at Les Combarelles. We found that Leroi-Gourhan had not indicated certain animals and signs that were on Breuil's earlier map, and that if all of Breuil's were added, along with at least two dozen engravings that Archambeau has discovered, Leroi-Gourhan's thesis made no sense. This has made me distrust his data for the other sixty-four caves mapped in his *Treasures of Prehistoric Art*. Beyond the empirical data itself, the thesis of sexual pairing is reductional and staticizes what in my experience is a tremendous sense of mobility and unpredictability in cave art.

Before returning to the Dordogne in 1978, I read an essay, later published as a book, by the archetypal psychologist James Hillman, called "The Dream and the Underworld." Hillman was not concerned with prehistory in this work, but what he had to say about dreams and the way we have used them suggested a way for me to begin to think about cave art.

According to Hillman, modern man has interpreted his dreams and seen them as a reflection of daylight and daytime activity, thus denying them an autonomous realm, an archetypal place that corresponds with a distinct mythic geography—in short, an underworld that is not merely a reflection, i.e., a diminution, of an empirical sense world. I was astonished. This was exactly the same kind of interpretation that had been cast over the paleolithic painted caves! Like Plato's allegory of the cave, the caves themselves had, since the discovery of prehistory in the mid 19th century, been thought of as containing a blur of shadows in contrast to a "real" world blazing in at a distance from them.

It was not a matter of merely reversing such a verdict, but of acknowledging that the mysterious signs and animals which originated what might be called "the history of image" may very well represent the forging of the way to dream and image as such a way is conveyed to us today. In this way the signs and animals become a language upon which all subsequent mythology has been built, and the distinction between history and prehistory starts to look like the distinction between poetry and prose at the beginning of the 20th century.

I have been led to believe over the past few years of thinking about this, that it is not Dante's shoulders on which poets stand, but the shoulders of Neanderthal and Crô-Magnon men, women, and children, who made the nearly unimaginable breakthrough, over thousands of years, from no mental record to a mental record. Of course they were affected by all that was in and around them, and undoubtedly they brought their desire to live, i.e., to kill, eat and wear animal, into the depths of the caves. But the work on the cave walls has behind it a much more formidable crisis than depicting game.

When I crawled for four hours in Le Portel, or Les Trois Frères, glimpsing outlines of isolated animals (with only several exceptions no hunter/animal juxtapositions occur until *after* the upper Paleolithic period), wounded once to forty times—or crouched before massive "friezes" of hundreds of entangled animal outlines spanning thousands of years, often scratched on one great bison outline, as if the earth were seen as a ripe pelt of animals—and saw within this labyrinth little half-human animals beginning to appear, more often than not as mere dancing bits—I knew that "sympathetic magic" and "sexual pairing" interpretations only skimmed what had been recorded. I felt that I was witnessing the result of the crisis of paleolithic people separating the animal out of their thus-to-be human heads, and that what we call "the underworld" has, as its impulse, such a catastrophe behind it.

Which is to say that Eden, which most people regard as a primordial image, from the viewpoint of paleolithic art is the end of a truly primordial condition in which what is human and what is animal are bound together. It is possible to follow their separation as it is recorded in imagery. At around 15,000 BC, a figure popularly referred to as the "dancing sorcerer" was engraved and painted in the "sanctuary" at Les Trois Frères. Wearing the antlers of a stag, an owl mask, wolf ears, bear paws and horse-tail, a human appears to be dancing—or is he (he is male, with an animal-like penis) climbing a tree? Is he a shaman—or is he a Covering Shaman, the prototype not only for Shiva but also for the Covering Cherub? The armature of this figure is clearly human, yet his surface is stuccoed with a patchwork of animals. As we come forward in time, we can observe the animal anatomy falling away, until with the early Greeks most of the deities are sheerly human-looking, with animals as consorts—or in the case of some of the chthonian figures, such as the Medusa, bits of other kingdoms remain, like snakes for hair or tusks for teeth. It is possible in the case of the Medusa to imagine the snakes encircling her face as the winding corridors of a cave, and the tusks, in the center of her face, as the ghost of that dreadful encounter where in total blackness and at times more than a mile from the cave entrance a human met a 12 foot cave-bear.

By the end of the 18th century, in the "civilized" Western world, the "shaman" has lost even a consort relationship with the animal. In William Blake's "Glad Day," the shaman/poet displays himself naked and free of all animality, his left foot treading on a worm while a bat-winged spirit, symbolizing evil, flies away.

*

The poems in *Hades in Manganese* were completed between January 1978 and April 1980, although I began work on the manuscript in 1974 when I first visited the Dordogne.

I was tempted to make two sections out of the book, one for poems dealing more or less directly with paleolithic imagery and one for poems which do not. Then I realized that such a division would be against the way I try to write. I have no interest whatsoever in writing poems "about" the caves, or even doing poems that can be identified as "poems with the paleolithic as the subject." It is the present itself, with all its loop backs and deadend meanders, that is precious to establish. The meaning of paleolithic imagination that I spoke of before becomes a contour in my own poetic thinking precisely because we no longer live in Darwin's everglades. Species are becoming extinct and threatened while I write this. It is because the diverse fauna-flora fabric is really thinning out, that these first outlines—jabbings, gougings, tracings, retracings etc.,—become especially dear, not as reflections, as I have argued, but as primal contours, shapes of first psyche, when Hades was a conjunction, say, of a bear paw buried in a hominid brain.

I always hesitate to explain what I think I am doing. I do not think that poets should do this. It robs the reader of his active participation in the poem. But I want to say this here: I have kept these poems in chronological order because of the way that the paleolithic focus ramifies, branches out, develops, then bends back in, goes with the main current, branches out again, etc. Given any focus at all, its repercussions are valuable. Once I began to concentrate on Hades, I realized that I was also taking on Hell, and that they were not the same but that they were incestuous, antiphonal. So it makes sense to me that after the first push into prehistory towards the paleolithic, culminating in the title poem to this book, that several of the following poems are obsessed with Hell.

As for the title: to conceive Hades in manganese is to take the Greek god of death and the Greek underworld and imagine them as having first been prefigured in black manganese dioxide by Crô-Magnon people. All of the black art in the caves is done with manganese dioxide mixed with clay, animal fats, and possibly blood. The yellow, tan, and red signs and figures make use of ochre.

"Our Lady of the Three-pronged Devil" ties the earliest sexual signing ( ) into its reactive development, the trident ( ). Under such a connection, there may lie the closing of this female sign, so that what was originally open becomes, at the point that fucking and pregnancy were linked, an oroborus enclosing germination. According to the way I am thinking here, the oroborus is hardly "prior to any process, eternal" (Neumann à la Jung), but rather a major arrest of movement which draws into its vortex an overwhelming preoccupation with mother goddessing the earth. The earlier open sexual sign evokes a labyrinth with an exit and stresses, sexually, torsion. It is possible that the earliest fucking/pregnancy connection was torsion (fire-making) and that the subsequent oroborus is associated with agricultural (as opposed to hunting) peoples, with the stress on the enclosed seed, the male as star, i.e., patriarchy in contrast to an earlier more mysterious "open" union, in which the feminine was place-of-fire *and* phallus (the so-called "Venuses" fit neatly in the hand).

By beginning to look at paleolithic cave art from the viewpoint of simultaneous psychic organization and disintegration, I hope to be extending our sense of "gods" and imaginative activity way beyond the Greeks, so that human roots may be seen as growing in a context that does not preclude the animal from a sense of the human. Up to this point, I have spoken of the crisis behind the making of what we call art as involved with the hominid separating the animal out of himself. To brood on this leads to several corollaries which do not necessarily follow. The size of the vast majority of paleolithic cave paintings, and the cramped circumstances in which they were executed, also suggests a drawing close of the animal depicted, as if the drawer were not only projecting an image but using the cave wall as a sort of microscope to work on and therefore examine the process of doing such work as well as considering what it came to.

The fact that many of these bison, deer and horses, and occasionally human figures, are struck again and again with lines that look like arrows or lances (or possibly ferns—or fern/lances, ambivalent plunges/

withdrawings, desires hooked on kill *and* live), suggests a testing of the drawn image, a wonder in attempting to make "it" go away—can I kill what I have made? Or, given the line/dot arena of an animal outline, can I gouge, in its rock interior, a deeper significance? Can I break through, given this ally, the substance in which I find myself hardening? Can I as bone/man make in rock a relief/island image of an earlier hominid branchiation? I set bone to rock in this question, as a kind of stone/flint fire friction, as if these engraved turns and twists were attempts to ignite a deep memory of Crô-Magnon's ape stem. There were no apes, of course, in the French and Spanish areas where the caves were marked and painted.

My writing in the present book begins to envision the root ends of certain Humanistic divinities—such as Hermes, whose first appearance may be a meandering line looking for something to bind that, throughout the upper Paleolithic, is found in dots, dotted lines, solid abstract lines, and the more complex "closed" signs, traditionally referred to as claviforms and tectiforms. If Hermes is a god of boundaries, it may be possible to detect his archetypal activity in the earliest boundary signalling available to us today.

Recently, Gary Snyder wrote to me: "The '50s-'80s was the discovery of the depths of Far Eastern religious thought for Occidentals. The '90s should be the period of the beginning of the discovery of the actual shape of early Homo Sapiens consciousness: for both Occidental and Oriental seekers. A profound new step. Knowing more of the Paleolithic imagination is to know the 'Paleo Ecology' of our own minds. Planetwide human mental health in the twenty-first century may depend on arriving at these understandings. For it is in the deep mind that wilderness and the unconsciousness become one, and in some half-understood but very profound way, our relation to the outer ecologies seems conditioned by our inner ecologies. This is a metaphor, but it is also literal."

To which I would respond: the Hell in oneself, and its Hadic basin, must ballast the poem as it capsizes or brims.

—March 25, 1980,
Los Angeles

HADES IN MANGANESE

Waiting, I rest in the waiting gate.
Does it want to pass my death on,
or to let my dying pass into the poem?
Here I watch the windshield redden
the red of my mother's red Penney coat,
the eve of Wallace Berman's fiftieth birthday
drunk truck driver smashed Toyota,
a roaring red hole, a rose in whirlpool
placed on the ledge of a bell-less shrine.
My cement sits propped against the post.
To live is to block the way, and
to move over at the same time, to hang
from the bell-less hook, a tapeworm in the packed
organ air, the air resonant with fifes, with mourners
filing by the bier resting in my hands,
my memory coffer in which an acquaintance is found.
Memory is acquaintance. Memory is not a friend.
The closer I come to what happened,
the less I know it, the more occasionally I love
what I see beyond the portable
gate in which I stand—I, clapper, never free,
will bang, if the bell rope is pulled.
Pull me, Gladys and Wallace say to my bell, and you
will pass through, the you of I, your
pendulum motion, what weights
you, the hornet nest shaped
gourd of your death, your scrotal
lavendar, your red red glass crackling
with fire embedded mirror. In vermillion and black
the clergyman arrives. At last
something can be done about
this weighted box. It is the dead who come forth
to pull it on. I do nothing here.
When I think I do, it is the you-hordes
leaning over my sleep with needle-shaped
fingers without pause they pat

my still silhouette which shyly moves.
The lich gate looks like it might collapse.
Without a place to wait,
my ghoul would spread. Bier in lich,
Hades' shape, his sonnet prism reflecting
the nearby churchyard, the outer hominid limit,
a field of rippling meat. I have come here
to bleed this gate, to make my language fray
into the invisibility teeming against
The Mayan Ballcourt Of The Dead,
where I see myself struggling intently,
the flux of impact, the small hard
rubber ball bouncing against the stone hoop.

Self-purgatoried in a cunt hexed mirror
he wandered off—"Come back!" the meadow
in the mirror kept calling, where he had not
seen his face but an otherness, in folds,
Niaux, a huge cave had opened up
where he was standing, but he didn't fall,
for he was already at the bottom of a shaft,
obsidian, and above? Floors of floor
lamps, all turned on, since outside the store
it was perpetually raining.
The air was encysted with Freudian shapes,
the life had been taken from bowl, or pen,
the earth so long denied now turned its green
feelers in, prefabricated yang and yin,
but from where did the energy come that kept
him in such purgatory? There, he knew the sun
would always be, active in his mind, no more
than floors of floor lamps lit, haloed by rain,
which stood for universe, one switch,
an apocalyptic purgatory in which the childhood
elevator swam, and the water lights
were always a thickness away, so that a meadow
could beam through, but be immediately chastened,
reduced to that vexed sore point in his palm.
But the energy? I cannot answer that, he kept
saying, perhaps the only answer is why
do I constantly find myself before a mirror,
as if one were set before me, its base fixed to
my shoulders like a drive-in tray to a car—
of course no actual mirror was there, rather
he had turned the object of his focus into a mirror-
like reflectingness, he saw through, in that sense,
nothing, though the effect was comic,
eyes, a beam through the wall into the criminal lair
where mother under father was twisting the sinews
of meadow, that he saw in the mirror? It was all

too complicated—nature seemed to mean:
go through, but before him the cluster of stop
eat yield and loan signs sent neon shivers
into the most distant spore. Something seemed to be
reorganizing under rocks—or was that just more
mirror focus? Mere fuck us, he heard, sea
leech from our pores the bottle-caps as well as
the glue of Florida nights, but once by the sea
mere fuck us fled, there was only brute water
without mirror focus to keep Okeanos bound.
By the stinking beached seaweed he could only
wish for the warmth he felt might be through
the yellow pane in the cottage overhead—
and where would that lead? A face would have to
open the door, he could not just fly straight
through the door-opener to the solution of
a telltale bed. So it was person after all
that gilded his purgatory, that magnetized
his mirror focus to whatever he sought to see
through, and the purgatory itself? The space
between: was the wetness reorganizing under
rocks or was something under his mind a coiled
python protecting her eggs? He considered
penetrating a woman, but was afraid the eggs
would hatch right in the act, then what would
be over him? Yolk? Little green pythonettes?
Again the sauce reduced out, yet the image of
woman as essentially only a pylon held, and
through her? Nirvana? Knowing was paraphernalia,
he just wanted her to gate, mirror focus,
gate, mirror, he got closer and closer to
what lies under mere fuck us, mire, fucus, then
the process muddied, the nothing that is
was now such a swollen bag, a wheelbarrow
in which he carried the immense actual
weight of his life, made weightless,
a maid in waiting, an insatiable glade.

Niaux is an enormous cave in the French Ariège district, a bit south of Foix, famous for paintings of horses and bison done around 12,000 BC.

Suppose I find myself, in a graveyard. Suppose death's presents are covered with black cloth, carefully folded and tucked so that in no way may the stone be seen. Do these shrouds mean that the headstones themselves have died? The dead—where are they? Japan, 1792. Behind the donjon at Hikone Castle, in the raked courtyard, a samurai takes his place on the seppuku platform. Instead of white silk, the square of tatamis is covered with black cloth. Before him, a small wood altar cradles a knife. The retainers tense. It is always the moment to emerge from life alive and there is no silence. The wind may die but its dying continues until, we say, the wind is rising. Died, dyed. The river cuts the sky and shuffles it. Black gargles all colors at once. We want to know why. Clotho answers, spinning. Or it is her shuttle answers. Or her name. Thread by thread, the cloth answers itself. A white stone leans against a black one. In the white, a figure is meditating on the black. If he clutches his guts, he will only work himself deeper into the answer. We need to set something before us, if only to understand how we are hardly here. A bird sounds across the accordion's drawn out branches. Each scream is one of the letters that name us. Of what is the alphabet composed? Pitch. Wind bells. A shaman's improvised bird-song. "Song," a dilution of his cri-cri, his kuk, wssh, the sound of wings, in-motion-words, grindings in the mortar of sound-band. The letters inside are hard. They want to prance, to speak themselves serpent by serpent out. We have a chance. To one side—Clotho. To the other—Atropos. We need to set our fate before us. To do so is sublime. Our heads, sometimes transistor stones, stones sister to headstones, sometimes we can alter what once upon a time had the covers drawn up to its chin. Or is our childhood the one thing we do not alter? Is that what death presents us with? I file, I fold, from having fallen. The bruised knee retains. The sidewalk goes off, its tale between its cracks. Or has its texture alone changed? The walks between death's presents are also covered with black cloth. I must not smudge them. I must spin my own thread, chance a pattern and knowing where to snip, tie in that moment one strut of what lost to myself I master.

Bob Cato (1923–), an American painter and collagist, designed the book which the University of California Press published of my and José Rubia Barcia's César Vallejo translations in 1978. Reading Vallejo inspired Cato to do a series of constructions made with black silk covered mats and doles, which he calls "Vallejos." It is to these "altars" that the poem responds.

Where I come from
is the accident's business . . .

exactly, how it made
thirty-five bone grafts
out of my impaled investment.
My dear father is here, not
off photographing monuments,
which he did so well,
in spite of epilepsy,
he took some
of the terror when the streetcar
created me. How those of us,
determined by one thing,
come forth
is no less complex
than you who are multifoliate.

My face unpacks
the corner of Cautemozin and Tlalpan highway,
"a simple bonze
worshipping the Eternal Buddha,"
van Gogh's words, that other
dear epileptic, whom I took to bed
in honor of my father.
I let both repose me—
I lead with my right cheek
thus profiling the left.
For a moment, I was seated
straight up in Vincent's chair,
and because the light behind me and
my body were infested
with incombustible sulphur,
I am sister to a double putrifaction.

We who are singly determined

we too dream toward paradise
even though our outpour is contractive,
"one dimensional," you say,
"she only paints one thing,"
you, do you paint anything? And if
you do, is your ease
hard enough to skate? And if it is,
do the figure eights of your admirers ever
come to more than arabesqued return?

My face is rubbed
back into the shaft of human
bluntness. Its point
is to tamp seed
into eroded furrows of pain,
to look back at this life to say
exactly what the soul looks like,
exactly what life looks like,
exactly, what death!

And I garnish,
fulminating with arachnoid thread.
What I collar and webdress
weights an exterior out and out,
worn Coatlicue rememberings,
scabbed twistings in the flannel of rock,
I was so handled,
such a sugared skull,
I lived through carnivals
of my own organs, a cornucopia of processed fowl.

The others were off rutting in a firework haze.
I was lobstered in my chair shell,
balancing my vision on the spinal
crockery strewn about me,
shards of an exhumed prayer.

I drew paradise up close about my shoulders,
I gave monkeys my shoulders as well as my breasts,

I let them look through your eyes to Breughel
where Flemish scapes fade back to Job
under a spreading oak, the Adamic Job,
amphibious, caressing his progeny
(As Diego lowered, segment by segment
upon me, khaki and emerald
Behemoth mottlings dressed my injury).

I know the dry riverbed of illness
where orgasm's rachitic child
crawls in place birthing
litters of female-headed moths buffeted by male-headed flames.
Would I be willing to allow both
equally to decompose,
equally to become androgynous,
would I be willing to allow my taper to become ant-hill,
my identity a sticky mass?
To no longer attend those mystical
pariahs, my sexual ties?

Yes, for parthenogenetically,
out of the emptiness right under my heart,
I threw up a collapsed
tent rising wet brown monkey with my face!
Out of the cave of inner nurture,
where animal conception could have been,
I connected my muzzle
beam to my snout post.
Gamy iodine on a silver plate,
I transformed the hospital linen
into more than a daguerreotype of paradise.

Pray no more for me, Mother of Unending Lightning—
illuminate the bleeding pulqueria nips
where gaiety, slaughter equidistant,
shishkabobs the sun
through a cellular catacomb of moons in
the quilted night sky pulsing

with El Greco bellows. Under the Mass
are the vast lamb wafers in the Mexican kiln
slid in at 4 a.m. on Christ-crusted rays.

I am fused to the inability to
reproduce what does determine me
with its unborn baby hand
which I finally learned to wear as earring in
the Galapagos Trench pressure
outside within what our species has lived.

Frida Kahlo, a Mexican painter (1920-1954), when fifteen years old was impaled on a metal bar in a street car accident, and never fully recovered. Until her death twenty-nine years later, she was in and out of hospitals, having some thirty-five bone grafts, spinal fusions and other surgery. In her painting, she fused Mexican folkloric motifs with French Surrealism and painted the most powerful self-portraits since van Gogh. She was married to Diego Rivera. An excellent presentation of her life and art by Hayden Herrara can be found in Art Forum, *May, 1976.*

SOUND GROTTOS

for Bernard Heidsieck

Out of a cove an animal
is always drawing itself, a night elope
with stingers buried in sound,
a nail wandering headlessly, a story
laked with frets, the stadium on both knees
inching chorusward, kale or Nile
we must not be afraid of norton, of
the nail in sound that cows under,
what a feel pound dogged by a cat lake savior!
I group by a well I inch the well lip I back
the dry nail upon which headless I honor
tor kay bain nie be tool
bank the river, the kneel sows to
the trail I am dissolving the hero, poetry with and
without organs, elongated summer
with its tree trunk tie-line, its I-less
Kwakiutal kidney lakes, a sorrow spun of seaworms, sound
caught desperately in bloomers, I-less
backtrack to attack the impetus that raises
me to I. Heidsieck,
the brotherhood is clapastropic, we must slum with hide and seek
cirrus, the non-infernal me pushes for air conclusion.
I like to tangle in the sail,
set the sail back to A Major,
the language is shot, buckshot, ragverbs, be-bes,
and it is very serious to sway core,
to feel our sunk hid ears heed
a man on all fours, pawing in place,
Nebuchadnezzar to wssh and kuk,
bicep-flavored tones, which
when tuned, yearn simultaneously
for syntactical yeast—how devegetalize
the language manger, hook out
the Hades-taming hero? Nada, the ghost garbed in our
essential boredom appears on the Noh bridge,

stepping in place with Nebuchadnezzar on leash
—or is it Death walking his caterpillar?
To shine in the dark
one must come from the land of the dead,
thus sores in the language now appear,
rents in the noun's sides, verbal keloids
taut enough to hold a rack of spiders,
prides of striving obscures, lions of water now
run from the gargoyle lanes of Saint Artaud, our Saint,
who from his laudanum cross held
o Zeus, o shining one, a crucifix of silver to
language's averted vampiric brow.

for Jerome Rothenberg

Anguish, a door, Le Portel, the body bent over jagged rock, in ooze, crawling in dark to trace the button of itself—or to unbutton the obscure cage in which a person and an animal are copulas—or are they delynxing each other? Or are they already subject and predicate in the amniotic cave air watching each other across the word barrier, the flesh?

*

At arms's length the image, my focus the extent of my reach. Where I end the other begins. And is not all art that genuinely moves us done in the "dark" against a "wall"? Olson's whisper (a prayer), "boundary, disappear."

*

Artaud's hatred of depth near the end of his life. All real action, he ranted, was at surface. Beyond—nothing; below and above—nothing. His desire to be frictioned into an egg. Organless. Eternal. James Hillman writes: "Every rebirth fantasy in psychology may be a defense against depth." If coming up out of the cave of night can mean an openness to knowing we've never left the cave, then rebirth ceases to be antagonistic to depth.

*

The beginning of the construction of the underworld takes place in paleolithic caves. To identify this "place under construction," I use the later Greek word "Hades," and it is there that the first evidence of psyche that we can relate to, occurs. To be in the cave is to be inside an animal—a womb—but to draw there is to seek another kind of birth: an adjustment to the crisis of the animal separating out of the human—or, the Fall. To be inside, to be hidden, to be in Hades—where the human hides in the animal.

*

Semi-conscious scanning through the lich gate, wandering the winding windows of images. Knowing that as we see through, we only at best see into dream to touch the cave wall socket in which the current is called *animal.* Its adamant muzzle confers moisture on my deathly palm.

*

Since the hidden is bottomless, totality is more invisible than visible. Insistence on a totality in which life is totally visible, is the anti-dream, Hades deprived of his cave, Satan attempting to establish a kingdom—or death camp—solely on earth.

*

As species disappear, the paleolithic grows more vivid. As living animals disappear, the first outlines become more dear, not as reflections of a day world, but as the primal contours of psyche, the shaping of the underworld, the point at which Hades was an animal. The new wilderness is thus the spectral realm created by the going out of animal life and the coming in, in our time, of these primary outlines. Our tragedy is to search further and further back for a common non-racial trunk in which the animal is not separated out of the human while we destroy the turf on which we actually stand.

The James Hillman quote comes from The Dream and the Underworld, *Harper & Row, NYC, p. 90.*

Le Portel is a trident-shaped cave, near Loubens, in the French Ariège, decorated with animals and abstract signs, from the Aurignacian period (27,000 BC*) to the late Magdalenian (10,000* BC*). Like the great majority of the paleolithic painted caves, it has not been fixed up with lights and walkways, but must be visited on one's hands and knees in more or less the same conditions under which it was discovered in 1908.*

Why write at all caves in,
microscopic men in concrete cold,
statues, pillars, risen
pistons from the underworld.

The dead, leavened, bleed
from the poet's body, eidola.

To sift the world is to pan
invisibles for their Hadic visibilities,
Hermic goldenrod, wraps of nature,
hollows from which elk still fly
and Hart Crane entrails us.

*

Hello to an idea: that as one's mind
focuses on the hidden
the visible becomes more poignant,
creased with its own spectral bloom,
its fly-blown manger,
its miraculous Noël, a fête of cold
where language, alone,
finds its way, word
savior sounded sorrow—

at the same moment
there was only this stretch of lawn,
an oak-backed corner of the Luxembourg.

I could not at first tell why cider
and swan appeared in my staring at
the lawn's concavity—it was with cave,
pregnant with collapse,
the underground was giving way.

The sparrow bouncing across the frozen blades
was a sparrow-shaped hole
zigzagging the shade, dark dark dark

dark dark dark

then it stopped, a sparrow again.

*

The dead man packed in meaning
must be the word otoko, hombre, homme,
of these words one's own father
is the stone, the precious
dull eye one fears may roll from
their ring, the spot in one's mind always
peered about, during the day.
The enormous father is no father at all
but the outline of an invisible animal,
a yearning on stone.

*

The animal father of humanity
a dog now heeled
by a huge hairless infant,
the Fall turnstiles, a windmill
interior throwing up and
throwing down, a many-meaninged
white in shadow, the invisible
tar of whiteness, a white man
with a squirming existence in his arms.

*

Behind the veil of Isis, the butchers work.
Bright orange spotlights overhead lend
surgical verticality to their pry and slice.
Behind her strip of serpent mind, fingers

probe the muscular pyramidic
tomb of animal emergence.

These outlines are not reflections of
the day, these crude processual marks
are not the consequence of, nor the impetus to, hunting.
They are figures wholly scored without their selves,
griffonage of Hades, anatomies of dreadful
hind confusion, anal sniffings skewered,
killing and rekilling image to see if an act
will go away, gravity suspensions,
paw raise of the first griffition.

Unicellular sac pressed
fingertips,

two dots, a me
row—or a herow? a meandering
red moist

blastospore, a multicellular
dot filled wall,
lubricious prefiguration of Hermes
who swings with

heat of the amoeba need
soldered to sprout

desire, an earthworm psyche
spiderline, tunneling on the leash of
the to-be-peristaltic

boundary seeking

something to curve
about, zigzag,
bear claw hut rain,
diagrammatic boogie-woogie of Hermes
flowing in the boundary catastrophe
when the animal was separated out

*

Dot, doorbell
summoning Hades through stone.

HADES IN MANGANESE

for James Hillman

Today I'd like to climb the difference
between what I think I've written and
what I have written, to clime being,
to conceive it as a weather
generate and degenerate,
a snake turning in digestion with the low.

But what you hear
are the seams I speak, animal,
the white of our noise
meringues into peaks
neither of us mount—or if we do,
as taxidermists, filling what is over
because we love to see as if alive.

Seam through which I might enter,
wounded animal, stairwayed
intestine in the hide of dream,
Hades, am I
yule, in nightmare
you weigh my heart,
you knock, in the pasture at noon,
I still panic
awaking at 3 a.m.
as if a burglar were in the hall,
one who would desire me, on whose claw
I might slip a ring, for in the soft
cave folds of dream
in conversation you woo, I weigh,
I insert something cold in you,
you meditate me up, I carry
what is left of you, coils
of garden hose, aslant, in my gut. . .

Hades, in manganese you rocked, an animal,
the form in which I was beginning to
perish, wading in eidola
while I separated you out!
To cross one back line with
another, hybrid, to take from the graft
the loss, the soul now wandering
in time, thus grieving for
what it must invent, an out of time,
an archetype, a non-existing
anthrobeast, rooted and seasonally
loosing its claws in the air!

O dead living depths!
One face cooing to another plungers
that went off, torpedos, in dream,
to spin through a pasture at noon,
sphincter-milled, sheep-impacted,
the lower body attached
to separation, pulling the seam of it along
cold cave stone, the head as
a pollen-loaded feeler tunneling
to ooze a string of eggs
where the rock, strengthening its yes,
returned the crawler to vivid green
sunlight that *was* profundity
now invested with linkage,
the grass, invested with linkage,
the whole sky, a tainted link,
man, a maggot on stilts,
capable of leaving elevation at the mouth
to seam unyield to his face.
Tethered, Hades phoned, om
phallos, the metro the zipper
of dread at every branch-off,
the pasture at noon conducted
by the bearmarm below, batoning
sun down word rust scraper by scraper out.

*

Below, in the culvert
behind the House of Okumura, 1963,
the conveyer-belt ran all night.
The clanking got louder, tore
then died, surf-roar, origin beguiling,
a highway was going through.
During late night breaks,
the itinerant laborers would smoke
by a sparking oil-drum in domed yellow helmets,
navy-blue wool puttees, men goblined by metal,
pitch black and popping fire. I watched
from a glassed-in porch, not quite able to see
inside the drum, wanting to engage
the action, to tie the fire into a poem
Paul Blackburn spoke on tape to me,
which wouldn't burn. He suffered savage men
without a context standing about a dying fire
jacking off into it. Depth was the crisis
I tried to raise. The surf-roar, earth
tearing, lifted, but not transformed, seemed,
as if part of me, an unending mechanicality.
I could and could not—it could and could.

I was, in spirit, still
in puberty, before my typewriter,
as if in a pew before an altar,
itchy, bored, afraid of being whipped
when we all got home. I played the hymnals
and black choir gowns into a breathing cellar
larder, a ladder to
convincing ore, a bed-shaped
Corregidor flashing, as if a beacon, to me adrift
—or was it the Phi Delta Theta dorm door opened
a crack? I would think of Mrs. Bird's canary
waiting to be driven downstairs and beat bloody.
That canary, hardly an image, helped me,
but it faded in an instant, the actives were
shouting around our bunks, beating pans.
Meowing like Raoul Hausmanns—or were we silent?—

we bent over where the wall had been removed
and only the fireplace remained, gripping
each others' shoulders our naked huddle
encircled the open-ended fire—we were fisted
loosely to a turbined mass, our heads
a common tampax clamped into the actives' hate.

A fire surrounded by walls of flesh is now
contained. Hades makes a target of this maze.

*

Perseus holds the written head out to the sun.
His sword from his hip projects what is on his mind,
a center torn from a center, Medusa
wrenched from her jellyfish stronghold,
her severed pipes, the caterwauling serpents,
his treasure from the underworld.
The hero will not be
transfixed into himself, he will lift
reflected terror from reflected depth,
he will thrust his hand down
into the sodden tampax mass where earth bleeds.
My father, for thirty years timing blacks
slaughtering steers, folds into men
beating the animal in other men,
extracting its Pan-pipes, jugular flutes of morning.

Picking the confetti from our hair,
Little Lulu and I cross the city
Francis Bacon mayors. In this city
cartoons mingle equally with men.
In their cruel goo outlines I sense
the terrible strength in our lifting up,
unceasingly to translate upward,
to take whatever stuff and lift it,
earth, dream, whatever, up,
the pyramidic impulse to slave-point sunward,
to streamline, rather than to learn from, Lazarus.

*

Surface is reality as is ascension
as is depth. Medusa hangs down through
fathoms of archaic familiarity,
the pylons men have made of female psyche,
women beat into gates through which to draw
the ore of heroic energy, to appease
a masculine weather for manipulation and torture.
War on matter lumped into a procrustian mater
crammed, with her crucified familiar,
into the entrance way to Hades. I knew,
holding my fifty pound mother in her swaddling
cancer sheet, that there is no triumph *over*.
Resurrection, a Carl Dreyer altarpiece, yes,
a true finger-exercise in hope, a waist-
hinge, in the waste of spirit the crocus-bud
surely is not to be denied, its yellowy flame
playing among the stones warms what is
youngest in us, most held in night, tender,
voracious for sunset, fire-appetite,
to watch the mountain smoke with modesty,
the thing to transform itself, lifting
from itself but carrying Hades as pendulum,
the parachutist gathering in Medusa's threads,
an intelligence under, not of us, but receptive
to us as we drift and wither. . .

Why do we treat the hero
better than he treated the material
he severed to feed the sun?
Perseus with his fistful of belladonna,
could we transform him into a hermit
with a lantern? Give him an awl,
teach him meander-work, zigzag wobbling through
the infante-clotted rushes, teach him salamander,
teach his semen how to stimulate fire. Unblock
the entrance way to Hades, allow the violet odors
of its meats to simmer in ice penetrating

advice. Something will work its magic against
the door of never. Hell Week, 1953,
a postcard Hades mailed to me,
his kids in demon-suits tied a string
about my penis led up through my white shirt
tied to a "pull" card dangling
from my sport-coat pocket. The personal
is the apex of pain, but without it
mountains begin to numb specificity.
The personal works in specificity like a tail-
gunner, the tension in the dog-fight tying
my death into my work. Airon is noria's
descent, airon begins with a shamanic
kuk and wssh encaged canary at the Chinese
box end of my baby-sitter's kitchen.

*

The poem is the Sphinx.
The poet infante risks teeing off into bluity.
Curl about the language thumb,
your hands stretched out to ocean induct well.
Concentration now includes Dachau,
barbed wire has replaced reason
as the circumference of energy. There is
no hail to rise to. Names are cultural
foam, pun wet-backs, nada-maggots
stretching their scrawl-souls, gnats
over oranges, loot-flies, paw
scorings in the frost of the mother corridor
where our faces were first ironed softly.

Hades receives meandering Hermes
mazing my thoughts into the La Pieta
softness of the target-maker's arms—
there what I change is ended, my despair
is nursed cryptically, for Hades' breasts,
like cob-webbed mangers, are miracleproof.
There a sucking goes on, below the obstructed

passage way, all senses of the word, stilled
in its being, take place. I am playing
with what is left of my animal, a marble
it rolls into neuter, a cat's eye, rolls back,
I crack its pupil between word-infant lips. . .

Bird spirit flew into Apollo—
animal appeared in Dis.
What was sky and earth became life and death,
or hell on earth and psychic depth,
and I wonder: how has Hades been affected by Dachau?
In the cold of deepest bowels, does a stained
fluid drip? Does pure loss now have an odor
of cremation, a fleshy hollow feel
of human soul infiltrating those realms
Hades had reserved for animals?
Are there archai, still spotted with
this evening's russets, stringing and quartering
an anthrobestial compost? Or are the zeros,
of which we are increasingly composed,
folding out the quick of animal life?
Is that why these outlines, these Hadic kin,
take on mountainous strength,
moving through the shadows of these days?

Color, coal whore, passing a million times
each night over the candle of my sleep,
negritude,
word prism in the depths of my lantern,
ice trolley,
fuse of sleet,
I follow your manganese torque,
your awl about yourself,
niggerness,
I now see how much I took from white king cock,
my maleness,
the nigger of my being,
the negro integrity in the lengthening trails,

the slavefolds in the word remember.

A wheeled figure stabs and sews
the infancy in our grain to the skin of the ground.
Wheeled wall master who mends in manganese,
talk through what I do not remember,
the life in which I am glued
stringings of narrative Ariadnes.
All hominids share a scarlet where the dark is
pitch with horizon, note-leaps, the static
of non-meaning tendrilling us, making way
for not another bringing of the dark
up into the light, but a dark
delivered dark paleolithic dimension.

The word "airon" is a neologism, a reverse reading of "noria," a Persian wheel adapted for raising water. The point in constructing the neologism was to establish a counter-motion, a taking back and down, from the personal apex, into mythic layers through which a connection might be made with paleolithic archetypes.

Fluffy, wet, stacks
on the ledge, falling on
in mind, collecting

the edge of a thought,
turning now not
as snow, but as a tear

lifts out from within
mountains
where no mountains are,

a loess transforming
loss, I am snowing
meanders, arrows, entering

animals, seeking something
to uncover, a storm
of plenty, homelessly

hidden in earth.

For one moment—one shawl—
I would like to relax,
a tourist. But the peasant's gold
tooth a moment later
is a hole smiling.

My mind, pained
by the certain pond
right below the heave of sacrifice,
adds coat on coat of paint
sealing the breath beneath it.

Yet like every tourist I worship
the unseen roads I thumb
desperately to eat.

*

The tourist,
the macadam on dirt,
the center stripe, as if to follow
were to range.

Yet depth clings to surface,
a bat to its ceiling-hold.
Without surface, this high-
heeled sheen of zona blanca,
depth is nonsense.

*

The cenote, turned on its side,
spills out the sacrifice
I had failed to imagine,
a crusted king, a gutted
shape of virginity.

What I roll
between forefinger and thumb
is cess, a precious sensing
when it wheels in me,
gold in technicolor.

Surface without depth
is flies on liver,
to the tourist a kinky tit to photograph,
a view of life as it really
isn't, as if rot
were the trick that draws the mass to sermon.
It is, it is an odor of jewels,
of maggots stunned into a tiara,
it is all these things, including tourists.

*

What I suffer, then,
bags in hand, undecided
before the night, is an ebony,
dark polished to tactility.

And the bitch,
whose entire belly is a sagging dug?

The exotic unclotting of death
pulls its bus-cord,
I descend to a flatter perfection,
lanced without scab.

Up close we are dots, lines, Louvres,
the sun is a specific human failure,
the anxiety to win. A realer light for
our faces might be an impasto
drunk on sieve, storm lowings, liftings of
Persephone endlessly repositioned
for an ultimate shot of rape.

If my words count at all, they are suspicions
that the news bulletin is true,
that a live rat was inserted into her vagina
and in about the same way
a coin is thumbed into a slot.
The new edition of Bluebeard has been postponed
—while Bluebeard lifts the eave of
Argentina, parks Nazis, leads
the ordinary life of Argentina one surmises
in a plane, passing over Argentina.

American faces are cold with confusion about what poverty
can be. A man in Harlem can thumb to Berkeley.
He will suffer, penniless, on the white-moteled road
but he will, if he must, get to Berkeley.
The Andean will not reach Lima.
He will end up in a barriada, one of
millions of earth worms begging from door to door.

We can sense the meaning of might,
the rings of rape ashift over earth's nickel,
the tortured Argentine, even the Pacific-
Persephone Hades is dragging down into his mantle.
But we are incapable of understanding Hades
coming a rotten egg onto that Andean's Easter.

Information on torture in Argentina from "The Argentine 'Model'" by Bernard-Henri Levy in semiotext, *Vol. III, no. 2, 1978, p. 109.*

The flats of the human face
will not admit (a mask). The ears,
jaws, cheeks (bent surfaces)
as they cry here mountainous colors
(worms), hurtled brows, worms of
mountains, husks of lean-to emotions,
arrogance dappled with
bringing arrogance closer,
gelid waterfalls of hares that do
not abstract out, but bronze, ruby snivels—

the flats, I repeat,
Marwan, whose peat rekneaded is
what Hades hides, our faces
the flat will not admit. The depth,
conceived on surface, is a depth I cannot
evade in mask. My leers, inabilities to walk
on a flat earth rounding me, reviling
Dachau months, they are available
because this man is not sure. Is not

surface, is not pure. Is
sink to the locust sensibility.
Eaten away, we are ripe, lame, the crux is
the human can be faced
but can the face be said in language?
Can a brittle alphabetic compost
zoom in on the hived
jungles cording Dis, the arachnoid trampoline,
the mast of bait coherent to another realm?

Head on, hand woven, a mandala of
tufts and thread taken apart, the human face
is a twisting warren, wave on wave of
tunneled crimson, days of napalm, nights
of azure peace. It is a kind of rug

before its shape is fixed—in Marwan's
works—in a between that is not
a mystical point between us
but a depth between the deathmask of the Covering
Persona and peeled off skin.

In this depth both mask and meat are included
in the impasto of pus-like fibers,
a rabbit flayed in a romantic gondola,
moments of unchanging plaster, streaked
by weeping caked with first fruits,
the cenote of the eye
limpid, greased by the plunging
flecks of things as they sacrifice
into our hollows, and our faces fill,
empty with passing through
and over, under Narcissus—

is it that Echo died and then
a youth fell to adore the labyrinth in water,
or is it that the import of what
we see becomes an echo
at the moment we reflect, and reflecting
weave on surface, milling this crisis
into mental walls, in the twist of which
we anticipate a face, more coarse more
animal than ours, a furred muzzle that in dream

begins to reassemble on our chests
animal grief entombed in nightmare,
pounding on our heart *Let me in.*
Not the fantasy of a childhood locked out,
crying for its parents. . . No, let me fold
that in, call it a minor green
but because it occurs allow it as part
of the supreme lock-out.

Dream muzzle wants in to a place we
no longer are, or only are in imagination,

a place so remote it is hardly part of our becoming—
more, it is the being
at the heart of becoming, the unchanging
kernel in the loosening hull of the human face,
chamber of the anthrobeast,
visible in these Marwan eyes, vaulted at the brow,
steeply recessing vaginal folds of stone
darken to the chink through which we enter Niaux.

Marwan (1934–), a Syrian painter born in Damascus, has worked for the past two decades in Berlin and has exhibited widely in Germany since 1967. The vast majority of his paintings, drawing upon the "aniconic" Islamic culture as well as upon such figures as Soutine and Francis Bacon, are studies of the human face based upon his own face.

He took the word "order" and let it go,
its friend, he strolled with the ripples of
its sounds and signs, ordure
he cried to the whirl of unrevealed
meanings laid out in the sun to dry.
His ardor was for a blackness alive with gleet
to sow in, to row a rock boat in a rock sea
making swells in the language, forgetting
the traveling, letting the erections in
direction speak spikes, be spores of
adders, get lost, be found by grappa-kegged cani,
roll in the snow of loneliness in adoration to
renewal, picking the staples from his lair,
being the lair here, feeling the red
in Dadd's old-fashioned root cheer, the murder
in the park, this too, with its undoable love,
is seated in the ark of sound, sound
chained to chound, unknown slave
at odds with its row toward liberty,
a mixed versus, the beginning of a web always
in warp, order, the warp in order, to begin a verb
he volumned her, she fictioned him, they
vertabraed each other to receive the Order of
Chrysanthemum, Yokohama, 1877, it floated
in their sake cup beside their bamboo Zero,
some ark, some coupling of a flower with death
gave us Narcissus, nah—gave us a mattress
hived with hanged-men lit alleys,
the edges of life swarming
with mythic ticks, we went underground
to inhabit enormous rock spoons, to ladle
away the climate of nothing, O lingam of sweet Raoul
Hausmann, you were stoned for displaying
your oak-leafed tongue, O sweet sweet leave,
the passage is sound, a yowling lore kittyhawks
the who I am alley, and of

the caterwaul I tomato seaward—Hermes butts in
with Catullus butting Zukofsky to clang
these horseshoe organs, a Chinese telegraphic
looped anagram of the language manger, here Oos is born
here Om flickers and weathers the King-Hadied
stars that droop with Lorca's sisterploys,
dear unframed minds of poets each
clutching their pieces of hemispheric
erection with its crocodile basis, the fear of
drying verb, of doors whose nouns will not turn,
of wee wee tethered kneenuts, alleyoops of traceyfire,
of nail notwiches mouthed by Gertrude, of garbage.
The explosion then is chestways, let me think
in Hades, No you cannot barter, Let me breathe?
Ah these catering badgers slipping off my coat
are Tanuki! The hung sake porter, the infinite credit
poker card peeler of nuptial asp-held pillows.
The implosion of garbage is a lopped event, electric
to the orm potential of leakage—let's count Hadic shapes
and forget that Hades is hidden, thus let's
count is oink and maybe, rank the tit with
the pores of Lulu spill, worm-fashion the word
assembles and desees its aortaed wimp, the last
tether of meaning, the bright burgher word,
is munched by Whimpy in the gases of dream where hover
levers of the tinker-drop nights we put the rock together.

To the buttressing diagonal of a gowned
woman's stare at a naked
man displaying his navel to penis suture,
a Caesarean Cupid opens his arms.

But no one returned from Kaufering.

*

A vase set amidst thousands in museum glass.
And in that thought, my mind drifts Kauferingward
to the Munich Schatzkammer, an ivory
snake-like Christ hanging, a pulled bow-string.
Was there an arrow? Into what did it drive?
As the metaphor stiffens, I feel myself enmired
—or is it cowled? Something is coming up about me,
a kind of confessional, a kind of protection
against "200 almost completely charred bodies.
The few uncharred were emaciated skeletons,
literally consisting of only skin and bones."

*

Christ has been drawn to the point that
in His image there is no more resilience—or am I finding
a new elasticity in making Him the bow-string?
Say he is part of a weaponry, that the tortured man,
a machine in which another spins,
is a kind of lathe now imbedded in our minds,
which can be used by any state. Say this poem
must bear the shape of this horror, that the Etruscan scene
must be held against Kaufering, as a piece of wood
to a lathe—how long? Until it is ground to nothing?
Until its contours, its cut-out hollows
become a testament, the vase in glass
infolding the Judeo-Christian agon that

after 1945, is so much mutilated scenery,
yes, but within the props, Kaufering's
typhus-infected marrow, dying in open holes,
the Devil's alimentary people ooze. . .

*

"the nothing that is" is injected with their souls,
this nothing dear to poets,
abode of emptiness and illusion,
where the veil of self is
for a moment grasped, grounding us.

Kaufering was a Dachau subsidiary camp, entered by the Allies in April, 1945. "All life in the camp had been extinguished. The living quarters of the prisoners were holes in the earth with a roof over them. One had to pass through a trench to enter each hole. The contents were more than primitive. There were no beds in the living quarters. On the floor there were wood-shavings and a few dirty blankets." This quote, from the same report by Capt. J. Barnett quoted in the poem, is from Concentration Camp Dachau, *Comité International de Dachau, Brussels, no date given. I purchased the book at what is left of Dachau in February, 1979.*

From the porch, nothing but mountains,
but in saying that, olive trees,
and the eyes brought to the multiplicity
of being here, in this quiet,
with the older peasant woman
sitting on a stone in the sun,
staring at the ground for hours.

Our gazes cross—hers empty
with the abundance of nothing to do,
mine fixed on what I'm doing
and what I'm doing is doing I'ming, abundantly.

In the palm of the mountain,
along its life-line, a village
sparks, one star, to me
on a porch perhaps a mile away.

In cenote black a nickel
core, a chimera-filled hearth
where fire gargoyles fire,
heart catapulted into

closed-eye-vision, zillions of
star foeti and I stand
the target Hades makes of life.
Does one aim, then, at fire?

Yes, but the minute gashings
of this corruscating must be
inscribed with the unseeable,
must bear a nickel that

must be said here. Must
is the way night demands,
its hidden target rings,
oval isolation and its pressure

to make. To express must, to
be in must in language, pressing
toward while withdrawing
meaning as a die balanced on edge.

Patters, paters, Apollo-globes, sound
breaking up with silence, coals
I can still hear, entanglement of sense
pools, the way a cave would leak perfume—

in the Crô-Magnons went, along its wet hide walls,
as if a flower, way in, drew their leggy
panspermatic bodies, spidering over
bottomless hunches, groping toward Persephone's
fate: to be quicksanded by the fungus pulp of
Hades' purple hair exploding in their brains.

The first words were mixed with animal fat,
wounded men tried to say who did it.
The group was the rim of a to-be-invented wheel,
their speech was spokes, looping over,
around, the hub of the fire, its silk of "us,"
its burn of "them," bop we dip, you dip,
we dip to you, you will dip will to us, Dionysus
the plopping, pooling words, stirred
by the lyre gaps between the peaks of flame,
water to fire, us to them.

Foal-eyed, rubbery, they looped
back into those caves whose walls could be strung
between their teeth, the sticky soul material pulled
to the sides by their hands, ooh
what bone looms they sewed themselves into, ah
what tiny male spiders they were
on the enormous capable of devouring them
female rock elastic word!
                                        They poured
their foreheads into the coals and corrals
zig-zagged about in the night air, to be pegged
down during the day,
                                    the animals led in crossed

a massive vulva incised before the gate,
the power that came up from it was paradise, the power
the Crô-Magnons bequeathed to me, to make an altar of my
throat.

Inside Staranova Synagogue,
deeply recessed stained glass,
such tender colors, pastel pinks, greens,
hammocked with cobwebs,
the slump in Czech character draped
by the Soviet net, the impenetrable dusk
our headlights could not shine through,
coal mine dusk, Borinage ghost of van Gogh,
a grimed religious body on straw
trying to worship its spirit up.

Imagine a living coal mine veined
across the land, streets finely
fissured with soot, a net become membrane,
a marbelization of the spirit
to which each particle of the burned
contributes. One says: the Soviet net,
then one smells and tastes the net!
A waiter explains why the menu's
suprème de volaille was, served,
chopped Chinese chicken: "Our people know
this is suprème de volaille."
Under the net, in ways hidden to me,
what *do* they know? Has the truth
in the life line marbelized lies?

Stunned before the vagueness of the sinister,
one's mind seeks out the physical world,
as if the mallards meandering the greasy Vltava
outside the botel porthole
has something to do with better.

"Don't start feeling sorry for a Czech,"
Milan cautioned, "or you'll never stop."

*

It is as if to think on Czechoslovakia
is to extend the soot, to describe
sensations, to participate in
a totalitarianism of imagination
which is description, the literal
ruling out the shades of place.
But if some facts are not given,
how can Master Hanus' address to his blindness
be understood? If the reader does not know
Hanus' beautiful astrological clock, know
that Hanus was blinded by Prague people
so that he could never duplicate the clock,
how could Hanus' words, spoken to me
in a coffee-shop, after I had seen the clock,
be understood?

*

Poets in Czechoslovakia are deprived of expressing
their pain, are made to lie to publish.
Where does the pain go that they are not expressing?
In the same way that I cannot forgive
the Nazis because I was not in their camps,
I cannot know the pain of deprived expression.
I can embrace Jan and Milan and feel
the extent to which the bow has been drawn
and sense the filings in the soot
collecting along the unsent arrow shaft.
I know another kind of pain,
the anxiety that comes from knowing anything
can be said, that cutting into is merely shaving,
the poet as a kind of barber,
sanding the druidic off the giant,
who considers who is to live in Viet-X.
You cannot speak versus
you can say anything and it does not matter.
What is not permitted

gnaws at the ears of those
through whom the able-to-speak
passes without effect.

Does the ineffable lie between?
Palm on a tree crotch by the ocean
Rilke felt the other side of nature
as a quiet, steeling bliss.
The other side of nature. . .
Fear introjected until the mind gags.
Shadow streets cheered
by eyes cowled with *I suffer like you*. . .

*

"For making time beautiful, I have been
pressed to time, toll
of the maggots stretching in my sockets.
By the ledge of the Vltava,
the heels of my palms press in stars,
chubby star worms unable to display
their energies along these poplar lined banks.
I made a harp of time, and hang
from its strings which they drew
through my eyes, a stilled pendulum
against the other side of human nature."

*

At the combined press of Rilke's and Hanus' palms,
something moves bliss to terror,
cancelling both, a kind of blister
in which a man in a Tusex store is trying to buy
his child something he does not need
with foreign money he cannot have,
a fistless man in a room without windows.

He lives, if life is the word, in stone draped with a red velvet cloth. Is he dancing? Dreaming? He seems to be turning itself, turning our view to the ram he is about to embrace. We are fortunate that he has been, for 13,000 years, available to a lamp, that he seems a bit pregnant, that much of what we feel he is is our imagining through ourselves a self for him, a Saint John the Baptist or "sorcerer."

Yet neither of these names is quite right—he may simply be a naked man, an out in the cold stone man with his right arm pulling the ram to his cheek, allowing a nuzzle to enter our idea of saint, the engraving of a long penis, without terminal, to enter our feelings for what it is to be stone, without any velvet to pull the ram down on.

*

Stone being is
grounded in an energy slower than our own,
a molecular drip, a hominid water altar
that Caravaggio smoothes velvet over.
The ram has been invited for supper.
Our warm hatred for the animal muzzle
is such a cloth, now worn as if
I brought my love about me and knew the moist
underside of its flayed skin,

"when daily and religious life were one,"
Artaud dreamed. Was he aware
that when gods and people commingle,
teeth unceasingly rend, teeth-men
whose roots extend to ancient
stump-men, tree-ring-men set in
tree-ring-women, no string leading up to
sunlight, they are gowned in a hand-like
wounded tarantula hobbling across

the ram's neck to pull down
into embrace the very Fall itself.

St.-Cirq is a small cave in the French Dordogne, near Le Bugue, decorated around 13,000 BC. *The most compelling engraving is a male figure with a discernable expression on his face–something unique in paleolithic imagination. He looks sleepy, pregnant, has very tiny arms and a very long penis. I superimpose over this figure Caravaggio's "St. John in the Wilderness," which is in Rome at the Doria Pamphilli Gallery.*

"Eyes glazed from long starvation"

                    Artaud's
pinched

two sides
                    coffee stains—

the rising
massive annihilation
extending its permanent

hair of Noh
      mange,
                    contains a sadness so
compassionate, a strait-jacket
                                        is blanket
over the rage

no cause but the chewed end

strapped to

      sound scrolls,

a Gainsborough "Blue Boy" scraped of human velvet.

This will not be read
is seen through. The attic
of the childhood home, the dear

things mother's mother wore are
here eliminated, fondled
once, as mother must

have been, behind a screen of custom,
through words gropingly
lost, a screen too porous,

words without clot ability,
a hemophiliac grain in elder
marriage. It swims up to

lie in the surface
quick of my language, this
lack of wastrel overflow, this

nameitsense, no imperative hurled
against nemesis
will make a wall strong

enough to nourish the live
inside of reader privation.
The Keep is empty. I am where

the reader should be. This too
is too simple, too responsible.
This will not be read

is the fault in which
I am my own ghost combat,
the extinct tiger, the paw-

ash-tray, grilled aura of
African savannah, the Sambo
breakfast, objectivist tiger,

checkered dada, smashing
an egg on its head, going off into
the yellow of its paleolithic

outline. Or is there too
much daguerreotype board in this
careful tarantulan walk, image

by image, across the void
I am trying to overwhelm, render
concave, self-contain, weight

with a weightless underworld home.

*

In my earliest word a feminine back.

The chute of memory clangs
atticly before her unseeable
front. Is she the unreading

reader? How fast such meditation
sinks to baby, how fast
the attic daguerreotype

backwinds to a crib on the grass,
the inquiring neighbor, my own
helplessness, empurpled and

austere with that stump we all
share, the waaah stump, the
night crawler writhing

half-uprooted at 3 a.m.
I do not want to be here
still convulses. No one

will read me because I am still a baby.

*

The attic must become a language

structure the master spirit
travels. And the infant?
The backturned reader shape?

They are the waaah and no of breath
that enable spirit to appear.
Only in maturity can

these stumps be imagined,
in a place below sight,
closed to human difference.

The infantile paralysis there
will not be released
until the reader turns

hominid, until we
becomes a nectar that scoops
under our sense of the human

and we bang,
note-dwellers in a strata below
race, at the attach

of the Fall, where all are
telluric and Cherub Covered,
swamp-bellied dragon-flies snarling

against our Siamese difference,
attached to
the hum of pre-poetic vocality,

where the human, twisting its
animal imperative, wrenched
free into narrative.

The turnstile of the Fall began to
creak. Lance-marked
again and again, immortality

tested, a few pulled the fragments of
their sex-steered, sex-dented
dreams out of the icy wound

the pleistocene sky had become and
stared into their dish of brains,
the psyche of underworld rock,

where the animal, licked
clean, was separated out.
The turnstile of the Fall

turned again. Hades
is therio-expulsion, a space
outside of which I put

my animality on what
will receive but will not give or
understand, will not let

me finger beyond arm-reach.
One animal line crossing
another is the greased ongoing

which no breeze extinguishes or birch connects.

Somehow it seems wrong,
a minute on Vietnam refugees
at sea, starving, not allowed to
dock, followed by a minute
on a new world's record in cherry
pit spitting, wrong because
the pit record trivializes a human
plight—so, should we dwell
on an imagined deck, imagined
cries? Somehow the dwelling itself
seems wrong, not only being here
but dwelling on what thought does
not alter. Or on what thought only
raises as thought, say my presenting
suffering to you as language
instead of handing you an actual
refugee. The baby wild hare
my son and I found had
abscessed legs, so we set it back
in its tall grass. Its tremble
brings the refugees closer, its being
alone, frightened, defenseless,
might enter the champion
cherry pit spitter's mind as
he dreams in a structure that includes
an altered sense of language
that must include the desert
mountains this morning not as part
of the news but of the evolving net
writing poetry throws out,
wanting to include, hesitant to
look back, knowing violence and
the moral impossibility of balancing
the refugees, the pit champ and the hare—
or is the poem to fictionalize such
a balance, is it to hang each with a counterbalancing

weight so that, clearly unequal, they
float over to an immense ear, an Ithacan
grotto, as the magical things upon which
the homecome wanderer rests his head?
It is too easy in a world that refuses dockage
to refugees to play on the spit out pit,
to allow the Odysseus of one's imagination
to rest for more than a moment on
an archetypal pillow in which hare,
champ and refugee are bees, producing
a distinct but unified Mass, an eatable
hosea, a surge toward a drooping prophesied head
from which flows a common honey
—tu viens, chéri? This structure
must include a sweetness in bed
as well as the mascara in the coffin-
deep rue St.-Denis doorway where the empty
champ touches the abscessed refugee,
where he mounts her in the hold of
a dingy, stranded before a lighthouse coyote.

If there must be clarity,
let it be opaque, let the word be
as translucent as night starred,

let it be deep with distance, and clear,
not as houses in moonlight,
but as a chair, window, ferns and wall

in late afternoon light are a clear
and dense mosaic, desiring
undermining, as if the mind

were steamed merely in looking to
where absorption begins, where the they,
unlookable through, draw in,

a venus-flytrap, my inability
to see through them and my perturbation is
enclosed, and more isolate, powerfully

adrift, my body part of
what I have desired to see into,
I do

go in as I bounce back,
the desire to imagine inside opacity
creates winding windows,

see-out-intos that keep turning
the word as a biological
being, penetrated, extends its feeler

in a long, seemingly open,
desire to be looped, utterly in
continuum, headless

gasping neck green in plant
contentment budding through lesions.

*

Here, what a word, what a thin
turn in and out of a no-space the mind
elects, a nowhere fleshed with everywhere,

including everyone, diaphanous as the word
"always," this here, chair set before hearing,
empty chair, colossal ear, rainbow that

hears me in, grotto of homecoming,
place in psyche where I look out,
dead, talking the life of being.

*

Is there not
a theriomorphic level in language

where the monkey in me gags the Clayton
and I either surface in elves or
write someone else's poetry?

All art, after the paleolithic, is
infested with complaint, that is,
all art aware of the animal

retreat in the word. You hear me,
other, but you are blocked by the person
you are hearing through, and if I

wave the listener away, only a hole
listens,

this is to only feel the sensation of
the soul, a not mine that is

neither yours. You

who I so desire to accept these poems,
you are the back-up
of everything I have had to overcome.

*

I am and I am and I am. Like cake
all day long, or crucifusion 24 hours
a night. To pounce from am to am,

to a.m. p.m., to enter the word *enter*
with smoking moss lamp—it seems
that the full ghost presence of the animal

15,000 years ago is the condition
poetry ever since has,
when it is wild with vision, sought

to mate to manganese,
where a tongue mired in I wheel
can't move

winces against the rational
afternoon, the bounce off bounce in,
eye to object, that sterile reminder of

what life would be without
orphan wee wee, the looney hues
that lather sight to the chord

climbers of the family vine
romance with which my ear and its honeyed
grotto, layered with dead, is rowed.

*

Prose turns back, careful of its straight

row. Poetry turns where
the where yearns, the yea

breaks. Prose puts hands on
the imaginary, guiding it to where,
like a plow, it tires of direction,

forgets going, speaks as poetry,
altering the plan, meaning serves
itself. Born into this winding window,

where birth and death are ever created,
a neutrality in the ordinary is overcome.
Then Hades says, "it is undercome,"

the image again crawls under urethral
embarrassment. . . Entering is
an infinite, fugal

straight flush, fully in conclusion.

*

Where the yea breaks? Always a piece
of placenta left inside,
agitating the opened water-moccasin

mouth, white tunnel of Persephone's
flower, the imagination is dew
silt bug and heaven burdened.

As a hungry man kniving grease
off tin, the human imagination stands,
this figment of my being able to

eat, this lie, the imagination
without its the, mage to in, at to shun,
a kind of final loss, nonsense

pumping nonsense, as if a mating were
at the heart of its is,
draining into the serpent's eye.

*

Poetry's function is racemose,
not to bloom from the urge of its stem,
poems are not cymose

but lead into secondary axes,
ox pulls in the genetic tick of grandfather
odor, a rattle to chkachk a bit of gravel

into the plate the sound in
poetry has become, gravel,
gravy and gravel, either too mammal or

too human. Nature now wears ache
eyed dice in every hand locked throw.
The gamble lodged in the word is Icarus'

penny feet still tinkling in Breughel's
arcade. The hachet buried in stone still
proclaims strike and be seized by material.

The gateless gate is down, the beast
retreats, oil spill is no more impure than
Mayan ghouls crouching in the calendar of

slave Tikals, but when the earth goes
so does nothing,
only the push toward definition holds.

*

In the beginning was the O, and the O
was so, was *oso*, the circumpolar bear
wrap, the tent under which first

"who" cowered. How speak into
the dwelling in which man is at
a protectional remove from fur.

Think of him draped in everything
he was missing, think of him with image
claw gouged between his eyes,

his teeth falling into his hands at
twenty. There never was such an O
other than in the mind that,

unable to walk straight through flux,
to live with instability as a fixed
mental condition, thinks back to

the umbilical rip-cord,
feels an O there reflecting an all.

For a second an image sets then
climbs into the roller-coaster car
of biological continuity.

Jekyll Hyde minotaur
right under human anguish, in the black
of the body where life is thoroughly

tarantual. What happens in venus'
flower basket we project into outer space.
But there is stapler terror in a rainbow.

Beginning and end should be the pillars
of a mental dolmen. Then why
do they lean, as if inside our temples,

against unbreakable O?
The beginning stays to the left,
the end to the right, I never leave the window.

*

Take this intercourse and let it wind
back to previous being,
suffering landed dryness,

eating its way back to
brine in the body of another.
To be born is to bear being enclosed,

to eat into a hearing, less a being
heard than ear tripping seeing,
so that sight falls here and finds

its limit. The image of an outline
vibrates back to its first
disappearance, fanged hand notched

bone. The primal grounding is
separation from that
which a person imagines to be his food,

or the outline of food, the enclosure of
no food, rock face, coldest food,
against which he craves, or chips,

thirty-seven times. What can he wound
in the rock? Outline is his arena,
his toro stab enclosure, but the bull

is not in question, no,
untouchable memory of separation drives,
repeats the hacking against

what cannot be eaten.
Once an outline is gouged, wounding
the rock becomes a wild satisfaction,

to daub wall, to try to bloody it,

to finger rock as if it were
the flesh of separation

is to imagine the unyielding
as having lived, a central satisfaction,
an intercourse I seem to rise off

but this I that rises does not
withdraw from having penetrated flesh.
This I is window to itself,

backgrounded, ground into its frame.

Bud Powell's story is never complete.
The image of a man playing blues
who earlier that day

sipped lunch on all fours
is rudimentary turning, crawling
chorus after chorus, lifting I Covers,

to view simmering Waterfront splinters,
he is visiting fist shacks,
the sipped milk becomes a dug root,

he bites into the horizon
wearing keyboard braces, he winds within
the steel cord all

who have pulled through mother recall
as the bastard spirit beyond her strength.

Convexcavatious day
in which life is undulating,

glassy white, under the bark of our
words for nature.

Who could say "beech" after 1945
without the dead in Buchenwald

turning visible
bowls within the words "beech grove,"

which are felled
as they are said, hammered

into wagons loaded
with the limp muscles of Romantic nature.

Flossing my teeth,
a certain taste
welling up through the tartar
os, the jaw where Tartaros is

chained being,
wine
sediment I am
a hive of
fumes on a string.

*

Siccity.

*

Salamander is conceived in fire because it was one of the first to make the gill lung metamorphosis. Its fire is the extremely ancient terror of air.

*

A dot goes into meander when it can no longer contain its own space, when it seeks release in image.

*

Animal is Fallen Angel, ghost of a former congealedness which included—not included man—but merely included.

*

A man seeking to channel in rock a way to let the crisis of his animality flow—this animality that so beautifully had carried him away from crocodile. This man, by his animal outline on stone, is knowing he is unique, and he is also begging his crocodile to return, yes to come back into his scratching place, but is a wet monster better than a dry one?

*

Sunday afternoon I squat in my mother's arch, eating, the black beckons so I go, crawling to I know not where. The terror of crawling within my own shoulder space is exceeded by the instinct that I might fully crawl out of the frame my mother dimensioned me with—but to continue is finally to return, doubled back on my umbilical possibility, and it is on the way back, not on the way in, that I scratch what might be thought of as the fact that since I ceased being an animal, I have not known what to do with myself.

*

Nebuchadnezzar bulging with feline sinew, glistening feathers, those toes they look like claws—but what is this trickster really up to? Does he put on animality because his animality, while never absent for a moment, seems to be slipping off him as he crawls from Les Trois Frères into the Parthenon, becoming a companion, a consort, wagging along at his side?

*

The beautiful biological fix, the doubled umbilicus of the continuum we worship as birth and death, is to be spoken, and neither fined nor allowed to go free. When it is, I know that my happiness is encased in the din in which one creature is boring into another. My happiness means nothing and yet it is, and continues to exist as I contemplate a hymn to those without plumbing or heat in the Cantagayo barriada in Lima. The Ararat of misery will always rise and be affirmed. To be Noah will always be dry.

*

Covering Shaman, you are the Tartaros-enchained Titans I approach every moment of my life. When you juggle my sex, tomb and excrement as desire, I talk Kali. When you crouch horned in the cul-de-sac of my will, I talk Minotaur. When you scatter my flesh, my son weeps Set. In essence, you are me with the abyss over your head, so that looking at another, I see myself through the abyss, and that other seems to be alien—and is, as am I.

*

It took thousands and thousands of years, but we did create the abyss out of a seemingly infinitely elastic crisis: therio-expulsion—and we have lived in a state of "animal withdrawal" ever since. The pictures in the abyss that flicker our sleep and waking are the fall-out that shouted us into dot and line and from which we have been throwing up and throwing down ever since. What we project as abyss, and into it, are the guardians, or sides of boundary, the parietal labor to bear Hermes, to give a limit to evasiveness, to contour meandering, to make connections.

*

Out of itself

the rock's
urine
yearns
coreward,

stalactite
in the hollow
of
my potency

offered to Tartaros
here, an erectectomy,
performed so that

phallicly
girderless

I make I
support language.

Les Trois Frères is a cave in the French Ariège, near St.-Girons, containing the engraved/painted "dancing sorcerer," as well as immensely complicated engraved friezes of animals and near-animals with an occasional bit-like dancing human figure. Nearly all of this material was faithfully copied by the Abbé Henri Breuil in the 30s. See Les Cavernes du Volp, *Arts et Métiers Graphiques, Paris, 1958.*

There is no connection between the death
camps and Lascaux. But what if the souls

of the living dead have been tortured to
the extent that no other abode could contain them

other than that cul-de-sac that by its manganese
ceases merely to be stone hiding, but turns

in the very word *abattoir*, felling or
hide of the cave, its fell, herd pouring across

a wall turned hide, the bridge I imagine
those hunters constructed from the seal of

themselves to the animals through which
they were boring—these phrases keep backing

into themselves, as if our condition now is
hugely umbilical, a gorged boa is our passageway,

something it has swallowed whole is the messenger
between the invisible and the visibly

cannibalistic, as if the cap of Hades is
a skull drinking bowl, and the brains I mouth

and the marrow I emphasize, that which seems
central within the rings, the trident within

Poseidon, the Jupiter within light, are contaminated
by the indigestible, this fish-hook I cannot metabolize.

The title refers to the human shadows blasted onto walls during the atomic holocaust at Hiroshima.

Lascaux is a cave in the Dordogne, near Montignac, containing the most beautiful polychromatic paintings of animals done during the middle Magdalenian, about 14,000 BC. *The cave is also rich in engravings, over 600 of which are reproduced with many drawings by the Abbé Glory in* Lascaux Inconnu, *Editions du CNRS, Paris, 1979.*

Her presence, art deco, ivory, half-toothless,
in her comb tonight—drawing
mother never dies
through a recurrent waking to
"no, she is really dead."

Mother is dead and
will never die. It is her death
that never lies. She keeps
on dying, so that her never,
living, beomes more mortal
each morning I awake to my own body
sure that she is not, here.

To say that she is dead is
to hear, between these teeth, that
she is, dead, and so she keeps her word
or, her word, vigilantly, is the guard
in the panopticon, and her valors
keep eyeing her, through the radial corridors,
noticing the Demeter
in Gladys, knowing that my mother
is a depraved magnet, drawing clods to
that site in memory I associate with her casket key.

Certainly, she is tuning
my sleep, only part of which belongs to
the man, I mean, the retombed baby i, waking, knowing
always too little, but to associate her with
earth is to offer her gender to the clod
stalemate I sense when I look at a turd on the lawn—

just let all these sensations be, but have the courage to
shape them. Call her on her bone, but hammer such call
into a clasp, the link in her compost, that she still
stirs, that if Gladys is the comb, the comb may

be attached to a chicken head, if she *is* the comb
then I rub fleshy ivory through my hair,
I shine my scalp with the pun of her, I part
mother to the left, earth to the right—
I look in the mirror and excavate the burial associations
from her sex, yet it is an ego does this. . .

it may be that Demeter
is an eye to eyeness with the earth, that if Gladys
is the comb, Demeter is the chicken head at furrow
with my gaze. And to move this prop away—
                                        the earth as mother
is a ripped comic, Empire State Building deep
memo scraps in my dreams. If Gladys is the comb,
if Demeter is the eyes below the comb, there must be
a wattle, an elderly mother-ladder into the cave
I so much want to be in, but to be here
as well, in such space mother does end,
standing there, here, I can see the wattle
tatters of *never dies really dead keeps on dying*,
rescue shreds rot apart,
everything that touches is a panopticon in sunlit grass.

A reopened carton of cream
whose encrusted top, left open a week
in refrigerator dark,
is the soul of a genuine nun

or the volcano held captive in the bell
of a water-spider. The deeper one goes,
the more truth seems horizontal,
and truth? A passer-by

who suddenly turns, pressing a whole Munch
Karl Johan Street to my dining-room window,
with his eyes on stems growing
from the backs of sickly lions

their whole bodies gnawing to and fro in the heat-
intensified shade of a microscope
below which Nagasaki still undulates a molten
ripple in the American flag by the dust-

moteless school window below which
the carton-children stand at cream attention,
their encrusted blow-holes evoking a depth
that is purely and thickly white

until their corpuscles are led in,
fly-infested, mooing, Charlie Parker skeletons
milked for centuries by the rain—
And now that we are all assembled,

to whom will we turn for the key to address
the key-hole, for we do believe
the sky can be opened and what the poem cannot say
appear, we have faith that all that is visible

can be concentrated into one highly potent invisibility

made visible at the moment we cease to suffer,
and all these visibles, then, blown away,
which is to say that we have faith in the end of the world

in contrast to the end
of setting an end into our tears,
repetitive magpie in the saline branches
of our infancy parked like a tree

in the seamless meadow of never zippered to forever,
out of which not only Gertrude Stein is issuing
but mixed in with her repetitions the vital
carbuncles of our carburatored lungs, black T-shirts

hung from the sky line, the veil that invisible wears.

THE AURIGNACIANS HAVE THE FLOOR

for Gary Snyder

Now I subtract myself from the industrial
white hive, a worker slinking off
from my queen valve position,

letting it spurt, knowing that in a moment
another will be plugged in my place.
It is Soweto miners whose 115 degree eyes

gleam from the neighboring houseside,
the studs supporting our king-sized bed.
I subtract myself while I add up

the multiplication that I am part of,
the scorpion-tail cornucopia that,
with nature disappearing, the earth is becoming.

A white American male, I am already on
one of its gyroscope grooves, zooming
the inner freeway of its outer wheel.

No, I will move instead into an ancient
squad at the cenote's edge,
having concocted a message for

the Aurignacian assembly.
What does not follow is
as valuable as what does

and now what does not follow
is turning away from us.
The clawless Cameroon otter, her entire

range endangered, waddles off
dragging a chunk of MacDonald arch
while Sammy Davis Jr. continues to yell

from the other side of the Beverly Hills
tea-cup we both inhabit, "Hey,
how 'bout a blanket for my piranhas!"

I feed the same peons in the same
meatgrinder that turns out groceries
for me, goldfish for Sammy's piranhas.

It is useless, at last, to complain about the world
all people make for each other.
Everything is owed to everyone,

nothing is owed to anyone,
a lot is owed to most
and something awful is due

to the streak of domination that somehow
does not become endangered in Shah
or peasant—sure, I know there is

a difference, but that otter would not agree
and it is that otter I am concerned about today,
wondering what she remembers

as she passes, as a species,
out of existence. I wonder if she passes
through the Aurignacian assembly,

I'd like to hear the speeches
as she presents the ogre intelligence
of her tiny arms where the sounds

are joisted with water-rustle,
presenting the black stump
smoldering in this new wilderness.

Hominid stump, in a vacant lot where
"something should be built,"
your center is hard "nor," ringed "neither,"

you are my essential humanity
and until I cease to blow my nose with you
I am your buzz-saw spectre,

the negativity inherent in
having forgotten the last glaciation,
that fiber I rediscover line by line.

When bison and I got on wall,
there was a tangle of wiving deadends
rotating in the animal layered midden,

pee-rings replotted by cross-hatching rain.
Out of the lovers' orchids,
$ mushroom secretes itself,

from the ground, straight up,
out of snowsporewhere.
It is time to let the Aurignacians

have the floor, even though we suspect
that the cup-shapes in Neanderthal
burial slabs are a fungus suggestion,

that in death a stem continues
to stalagmite, seeping through
the crack of subliminal scanning while

I try to step back from this stump
out of which, like a bubble-gum machine
scoop, a silken, rainbow, tar

and sulphur-woven ape hand is extended,
offering cholo for me to chew
on the loosened knot of path

upon path, bundled by the Buddha's
vatic Gaboon viper nature.
My senses must flee to the highest bison

hump. There,
a fool riding a mountain,
playing my turd accordion, out of which

Hades' purple hair is sprouting,
while my balls press against what
still confirms infinity,

I will accept the Aurignacian motion
that the abyss is engravable
and terminates in caves manifesting

hominid separation.
I dead is under
I do, lobster verb to lobster verb.

My vertical stands on my zero.
It is now possible to chip at the target's
dead center, the bison outline

by whose manganese side
I am painting the clawless Cameroon otter
with the disappearing silver of a Dracula stake.

Reindeer herds
in the black knight of TV, shining
in his armor, through his organless chest,
simulacra, on their way
through the new wilderness.

I stand in Aztec time,
the paleolithic is in the room,
deer dots pumping where
this knight's heart should be
—but his heart, it is
a million reindeer hearts
collected in the never
before so close charged distance.

The title refers to the lavishly decorated lava boxes that the Aztecs hewed and used for burning and storing human (sacrificed) hearts. The word itself, according to George Vaillant in his The Aztecs of Mexico, *means "eagle vase," and is pronounced "know-shee-ca-llí."*

Shield of the enwebbed dryopithecine,
this branchiating autumn,
God is the tomb
in creation, a voi dance knotting

the air into leaves
bound
for the great fast,
syncretion, a binding fast, to step

on the excellent heart of this muttering
void in creation, a syncretion din

binding sin to these leaves
bound for the great binding, each a fast

tomb knotting a boundary into
a web, branchiate
heart of this excellent
dryopithecine, autumn is
the creation in God,
a branchiating din of leaves, a binding
fast bound for
the great fast, each hominid is
a marked boundary marker dancing

the void into a web, the void is the God
in creation, a binding
sin, syncretion,
these leaves bound for the great creation,
binding each fast leaf to a scattering

boundary, language
branchiates on the shield
of the web-building dryopithecine,

to fast
on the boundary marker of creation God
is the void in each leaf, a syncretion

binding the great fast to sin
binding my dryopithecine voi dance,

bind this excellent autumn
step into creation,
the void in God's syncretion, a boundary
fasting in its very binding fast.

The desire for time to speed up, so as to get more quickly to the next peak, fills me with ash but also turns me volcano. I am fixed here. The peak I await is fixed there. Must be some way out of this, Jung thought to include the valley as part of the peaks, let it join us, be our greater sharing, so that the distance, felt as air, is shaped by a kind of extended letter "u," peak-valley-peak, or to put it another way, there is a pinhead staring out my eyes, and he goes down through me, losing me through the ground but continuing until he comes up in you.

I imagine that if you grant his existence, you do not feel that his feet are tangled in your head. You will say: "His head is in my head—his feet are tangled in your head." I feel the same way. The divine man may connect us, may contain our "collective" experience, but since he is reversed in all of us, we do not see eye to eye. Perhaps it is up to me to allow you to have his head in your head and to accept his feet in my own, to let his heels stare from my eyes, offering you the feeling that he begins in you and ends in me. Which may have its advantages for me too, for if I have to drag his knees about in my chest and constantly feel his ankles when I swallow, I may also be less compulsive about getting to the next peak. I may even learn a contentment to peak here, in the flat. Since I reach nowhere, how try to erase with my shadow the valley that one might say contains my greater part, chipped pebbles two million years old, before the pinhead, before even the flinthead. Something human in saying to the giant: "I won't hurt you. . ." Same thing in a peak, in the desire to pinhead up, to ego to a point, especially when, in looking down, I find that I am language-gnarled, porous to the moisture the etymological tendrils induct.

Can these peaks be grasped, as if made of springs, and the sound of the pinheaded ego released as they are worked back and forth? This taking hold, this working anything back and forth, penis or Fascist, is excitedly, and sadly, Aurignacian, for strings of river, sentences, are so many tangled paths through the valley, in or outside a cave. The mental thing I do with my body is to seize an adder handful, hold it mock-heroically, for a moment, like lightning, then watch it grasshopper off in forty directions at once to reassemble here in a grid that looks suspiciously square, orderful, as if the beginning had increased and the end had been dragged in. The rotted man, inside animal, is a cactus weathered marrowless but still upright, even though the root connection dried up seasons ago.

The roadscape in the rearview mirror is a postcard framed by the onrushing though more still sky, under which we seem to be slipping, as if we were being tucked, feet first at seventy, in the miles per years of Saint Anthony, the fist of a Grünewald monster the propeller in his white hair. There *was* a wilderness for him to enter, a story to contain what possibly only occurred in a didactics to control the static, in which wisps of him are left. The scene on the postcard momentarily reassures me: two Racey Helps bunnies have entered the tree theater for a "Case of the Missing Carrot" matinee. Neither animal or human, they were conceived to defuse the dark of the childhood bedroom with the consequence that it doesn't matter what we do to animals if we originally related to them as cartoons. As the covers of what is being drawn up reach our chins, we understand that the meaningfulness of framing a space where a bit of misercordia might be created and dallied with will always be truffled with the shrapnel of systems.

The rotted man inside, who used to seem archetypal, is biological and his "language environment" is amniotic and porous to heroin. He is the new wilderness announcement that there no longer is a wilderness which has not been mixed with non-wilderness. As an American, I sense the bit of sandpaper working at our floodgate pimple which, if rubbed open, would let flow millions of corpses and they would drift in the anxiety that America must be destroyed, that we are one of six in the lifeboat and eating half the food.

So I understand the arachnoid texture of the air I breathe. On my corpus callosum I hear the Buddha, a tapeworm wrapped in saffron, stepping in place, murmuring: "I was at the spot in the

Persian Gulf yesterday where the water was, for fifteen seconds, the temperature of the sun. After that, it is hard for me to believe in anything you write."

Spend language, then, as the nouveau riche spend money
invest the air with breath newly gained each moment
hoard only in the poem, be the reader-miser, a new kind of snake
coiled in the coin-flown beggar palm, be political, give it all away,
one's merkin, be naked to the Africa of the image mine in which
biology is in a tug-of-war with deboned language in a tug-of-war
with
Auschwitz in a tug-of-war with the immense demand now to meet
the complex
actual day across the face of which Idi Amin is raining
the poem cannot wipe off the blood
but blood cannot wipe out the poem
black caterpillar
in its mourning-leaves, in cortege through the trunk of
the highway of
history in a hug-of-war with our inclusion in
the shrapnel-elite garden of Eden.

Our Lady of the Caves
dressed in rock,
vulviform, folded back
upon Herself, a turn in the cave,
at Abri Cellier
an arch gouged in a slab
makes an entrance and
an exit, She is a hole,
yet rock, impenetrable,
the impact point of the enigma
"no one has lifted her veil,"
the impact point of the enigma
yet rock, impenetrable,
an exit, She is a hole,
makes an entrance and
an arch gouged in a slab
at Abri Cellier
upon Herself, a turn in the cave,
vulviform, folded back
dressed in rock,
Our Lady of the Caves

As She folds back
I sense a long sentence dissolving within itself
and when it ends, it is just beginning,
a presentiment that Her sign is
one turn, uni-
verse, end of a first line, curved about
a vaginal gouge, as if what is bent about is foetal,
as if She
is a foetal arch bent about a slit
that goes in one quarter inch.
Our Lady may be the invisible archwork
through which all things
shift gears in the dark, at cheetah-speed,
at snail-struggle, on the shores of Russia

where paleo-archetypes compressed into radar
gaze around with dinosaur certainty.

Before Okeanos, continuing through
Okeanos, before the uroboros, continuing in it,
Her gibbous half-circle tells me that She was,
before an association was made between fucking and birth,
before a bubbling parthenogenesis was enclosed—
but to what extent She is
in self-enclosure, in my beak triumphantly
raising my penis to the sun,
to what extent She neatly
slides Her slit between my self and its point,
I do not know.

For the self has grown so enormous,
I look through literal eyes to see Her
on a slab chopped out of Abri Cellier,
in a cool limestone room in Les Eyzies.
She seems only several inches tall.
It is a funeral to be there,
in a burial-chamber where first otherness
is displayed behind a rope, with written instructions
which only describe the age of a shape.
And I who look upon this am immense,
encrusted with all my own undelivered selves,
my skeletal papoose-rack through which my mother's
85 mile long legs are dangling, out of which my father's
right arm with a seemingly infinite switch trails
down the museum road, across France, to disappear
in the Atlantic, and I jig around a bit,
not because I have to pee, but because this ghost dance
starts up as I stare through the hermaphroditic
circle the snake made, so self-contained,
but what it and I contain, the "divine couple,"
is the latent mother-father who
has taken over the world.

Our Lady moved about
like a stubby pitchfork,
yellow fiber gushed out from between Her prongs,
She hobbled, toward image—
what lurked under Her vulviform was the trident
yet to come, for men realized that not only
could the point of Her slit be hurled
but that its two bounding lines could be too,
the whole woman could be thrown into the animal.
At Les Trois Frères, only meters away from the "sanctuary,"
is a huge bison abattoir. What is now sealed over
was a ravine at 15,000 BC. Was it because She
was nearby that this ravine
struck, like flint, "abyss"
off the rock of those hunters' minds?
And way in, trident deep in Le Portel,
did Her three prongs close?
Was the uroboros hammered shut
when those hunters at last hacked
themselves free from animal sinew?
And was this the point at which
the wilderness was mentally enwalled,
serpent the outer circumference,
to teach, and banish, our Adamic Eve?

Below Our Lady, on the wall of my mind,
is the foot long rock phallus Her devotees may
have taken inside them while they chipped in Her sign.
I have been straddling, all poem long, that insistent,
rapacious thing, of phallus, the tooth-phallus,
the borer, for the tooth-phallus is insatiable,
male hunger to connect at any price,
but not to connect, to cease being an island,
a speck before the emancipatory shape of
the birth-giving mainland, to build a mole
to tie fucking to birth, to cease being ticks
on the heaving pelt of this earth, to hook
their erections to the sleigh of a howling starvling.

And they did
get across, at around 10,000 BC,
one night fucking and birth were connected by a mole
burrowing right under the surface of a full moon
boring a red mortal line from the edge
to a point equidistant from the circumference.
The corpus callosum was suddenly filled with traffic.
The last Magdalenians were aware that Our Lady
had closed. They padlocked Her
with the uroboros and planted the key.

She now grows on a long handle
out of ground at the edge of the abyss.
Some see Her as fly-eyed radar.
Others feel it is to Her prong that they cling
as the gale of monoculture whips them horizontal.
Many more on their knees inch along cathedral pavement
toward what they believe is her virginal compassion
which will somehow make their manure-colored
barriada water pure, their nipple blood,
their inside-of-their-bodies
muscatel in which their children play,
miracle and misery on which my index
touches, to stir for a moment Her
gouged rock socket
octopus current of
faceless suckers Veil.

Abri Cellier is a rock shelter in the Dordogne, near Tursac, with deeply incised sexual signs dated at the beginning of the Aurignacian, around 30,000 BC. *These "workings" are later than Neanderthal gouged cup shapes, but they are the beginning of image, or the presently discernable point at which dot, line, and smudge, begin to imagine us. There are several such rock shelters in the Dordogne with engravings that pre-date by several thousand years the animal paintings in unlit cave recesses.*

RAMAPITHECUS

for Bernard Bador

My days here are inadequate.
Inside my own spine,
I can study chakra anatomy
or the relation of the world tree to
this Chaplin of a Christ
who, with his girlfriend Paulette,
must be shot down
the crossties to Hades—
but to merely speed up his waddle,
to merely consider fucking
with the momentum from too much talking,
will not bury me deeper in your mind,
will not pulverize my die
mixing its powder with the mental space
over which your thought is arched,
vivisepulture, that thought of me
in which you remain buried alive.
Think of my dice as lovers
tumbled out on the green—
what do their swastiky mudras propound?
I am, not what I say I am,
I am not, what I say I am,
I am not what I say, I am,
I am Not What, my name is Not What,
I gambol in the maze of the world
with the horse-power of Los Angeles,
the meaning of my die is more intricate
than what bonewise I seem to represent.

*

The poem will be gone in a season,
a manganese tow. You have a sow idea of what
death means: a Demeter plot, a crime before and
a criminal after-

whore, which I pry apart to watch you
rubbing the pus out of your skirt
as if the stain of the biological continuum
could be removed, and you could just be,
as am I, a nectar
without corolla or corona,
where the sun mates with the tongue
and a black spot begins to spin,
gemelliparous spore, at inception yoked
to the sun's dream of its own cinder
as well as to the centipede ballroom
where the masked workers hurry
in and out of the centipede queen's side,
in the roar of her tat-a-tat-tatting soles—
this nothing suddenly something,
my orphan wee wee, pubic
papulosquamos puppy seeds, p p p
then nothing, pugilist scent,
your pew-shaped smell in which my pfew
is already being lathed to furniture by
your coffin hone.

*

Your error is to conceive me
a hunched brown near-man
stoned on notching pebbles for several million years.
At least think of me as a brownie
or at least as the red spot in a Girl Scout's panties
or at least as a cake sweetened with currants
or at least as the soul of a pectoral sandpiper,
at the very least the entire density of any word,
so that the core of me, *casco*,
divides your isolation,
"helmet," "skull," "shard" and "rind."
At least, as you strap on your bra
cupping your hooves,
think of that centipede hoofer,
the hookup between breast and skull,

for surely you know
that my die is mixed in your milk
and so, as you strap on your skullrack,
please realize that your raised heel
only tilts you more into the sky, and away
from my concavity which is casco enough
for you to baptize baby Wallace
who, dipped in me, is not merely berry conclusion
but one of those who, suicided in womb,
is less caul than ally. What poet
really wants to hold up
the head of a beloved beforer?
Adolescent life-guard! Let him drown! Forget
before, let way before speak
the out-sized yearning that is
my poppy gist, my petal afloat in itself.

How clean, transparent and opaque
Our Father of the Caves is, at St.-Cirq.
How potential, how unfilled out,
a blank interior in which my eyes
can explore their rock, and not in black
painted but in unlit recesses where a wave I,
a tentacle man shaped by a dream breaker,
starts toward paradise, to let
the Father in stone writhe with the hallucinatory
skin of a "sleeping cherub," Caravaggio's
beautiful jaundice lime Dionysus,
gathering himself into his fawn cluster,
turning from us, as if to say,
"This is all that is left of paradise,
come fuck me for a moment, forget
you are fucking anyone, let even your flesh be
decanted onto the white cloth of your experience."

*

How evil He seems in urban light, set
like a pusher between the predictable,
if filthy, buildings. No snake will
flash from his unwashed skin. No jungle
to surprise me. No spooked me to bind
with a thousand taboos. Only one taboo:
you must not imagine a justifying being.

*

The origin of complaint was a perspective of
paradise wedged
between the primordial past and the present.

*

My basic exercise was to lie on my back, naked, knees raised, legs falling out and being brought back together in coordination with breathing amply in and out (at "out" the knees flopped to the side—at "in" they were up together) AND to stay in eye contact with Dr. Handelman while one of us talked. The more I stayed in eye contact while doing this kind of breathing, the more I felt my body—which led me into severe emotional corners. After a year of this exercise, with all its consequent meanders, I started to feel a streaming sensation in my feet and fingertips which, over the second year, gradually passed through my body to the point that near the end of the therapy a bracing streaming would take place throughout my entire body immediately after commencing the exercise. To be naked, on one's back, knees raised, under the searching eye of a clothed adult, evokes what is earliest in us, not only our infancy, but also being suffused with feeling and inducting and responding to whatever is outside.

The terror of selfhood is to enclose us and then pass us into the hands of its iron-maiden which totalizes the crucifixion. Artaud's words, "the unspeakable cruelty of living and having no being that can justify you," seem to be those of someone who has cut off contact with the outside and who is in the process of wringing the neck of innerness. "I talk the enwalled totem," he also wrote, as if to say: the sounds I make are those of my penis which I have sucked up inside me and ossified.

*

My dreaming Crô-Magnon,
how other he might have felt from bison.
Might he have drawn bison to induct a mystery
far more distant than the animal is to us today?
Where do the extinct species go? Into
us? Are we the abattoir into which
tiger and crocodile are tumbling,
as Artaud's "enwalled totem" becomes a beast
monument, a precious good beginning
to stir the water of a mothery veil,
so that I start toward paradise as

I concentrate "here" into a nucleus, binding
where I find myself, so that the ends of the instant
can be glimpsed writhing as if
from a central hold?

Life becomes
pure Los Angeles, and again a between
beams through the language, and it is with difficulty
that I keep dreaming, on my side now,
looking pregnant, but really only a man sleeping
on his side, belly relaxed, his penis inching forward
so as to provide a greater acceleration for his soul
as it goes forth into the night,
a cherub stretching to exhale
a disemboweled bison, the wounded animal
he has brought into what is human,
so that breathing now is
a billowing of this animal in and out. . .

O wounded animal of complaint,
even though you have no hands, use your hooves,
pack back into yourself the intestinal
topology you have, with my incision,
draped about the world.

Less to kill, than to map
the depth of the bison,
which might have been Crô-Magnon's Mars,
horse his Venus. . .

his first scratches, meandering lines,
might be paths put on cave walls
to make sense of the terrain.
In the tangle of Aurignacian scratches, animals seem
the result of meanders tangling and containing,
twisting, net-shapes with eyes, as if image
was a creation of
too great a path density,
a knot, what paths crossed for.

As bison and horse emerged in his images,
did he reactivate his hominid stem?
In this cold, was he
bent about the jugular of
unrememberable heat branchiating through him?

Dryopithecine abyss of what he was,
was not, countermotion in a bison's eyes.

Tonight I would be turned to word by her,
become sound enough
to penetrate her outstretched tongue doing
lalala to the night, baby snakes of laughter.

I have suffered long enough
the adder-draped skull
at the intersection of Athena and Medusa.
Tonight I will call her on her stone
to make a vowel elasticity capable of being
stretched across language,
to bound into you and feel,
in the force coming up from below,
the initial consternation
of her snakes becoming caves,
then to weep in the shape of her snakes,
to become muscular here, where the gorgoneum
is neither aegis nor shield
but every which way moving words.

My meaning becomes sound opalescent
and I plunge back into her laughter,
for the cuckolding cherub can never be rooted out.
The mantis egg sewn into my coccyx
is the philosophers' stone, the pavement
of the poem, stone crushable as an egg.

She was the war in me because my member ends
a mere hope inside
her warm gear well.
There is now no way to even pretend
that I can see with my penis.
The one chance that I have
to understand what goes on where I cannot be
is to take the focus of all my negation
and place it on the language burner.

When I broke off her lovely wild boar
penile fingers
and insisted she stop wearing shit for lipstick,
I deminotaured language.
So she *is* reflection—
let slashed neck run in mind,
a terror of the throat intact,
of the whole detached sentence,
of the predicate that is not suffering amoebically
to become clothed
like a bird, with wings for garments.

There is no mythical result in which to find her,
no location, no coupling. What I thrust into
is language, whose hollow is its pregnancy,
whose innerness, occasionally dripping,
feels like forceps. What I must grasp
is that nothing can
be drawn forth.
Once I have allowed this hollow to inflate,
beginning and end are unable to touch.

CIMMERIA

for Eliot Weinberger

One must have a mind of stone
to find lineage in cave scrapes meandering,
and to have been unuprooted,

for a long time, to express the ligament
stalagmitic to Auschwitz,
Siamese mitosis, twins who want to lick

the eyes off the dark, bereft of everything
but the silt in the deepest
gouge, one quarter of an inch, Cimmeria,

"covered with close-webbed mist,
unpierced ever with glitter of sun rays,"
where the goat-bodied Chimaera, the last

Atlanteans, lived, before the fangs of Hades
meshed with the fangs of earth. And now,
beyond? Abysses upon abysses of ice

in which fishbone-like groups of humans
are toiling at 15,000 BC, roughly
the midpoint in the history of image,

the hitching-post of the sun for who is
with cave, soon to bear an emptiness
that will open out and out against

the steel of this hour in which all
seems present, nothing satisfactory,
Saturn's factory boils down in the harpyless

churn where I, the anchor, is dropped.

Double pelican of Clayton and Paul,
work in which the dead nourishes the living and
the living nourishes the dead.

Clayton lets Paul
invade him now. Their lower bodies pucker up
to receive the shaft their heads extend,
a deep one, now at a 45 degree angle
into the earth.

"I thought I would write a poem exactly in
your way, your dō, I mean, your path,
write a poem in your path—but all I seem to be
able to write is 19
East 7th
Street,
or is this
your path,
your address
my speech?"
"Yes, if you are true to me, faithful
to the cooking" —and then he went over to what
Clayton now saw was a kind of stove— "you must follow
the poem as if it were a recipe
you had never performed, even though the in-
greed-
ients, the word grain, you handle again and again.
They appear strange to you
because words are energy deposits, blackheads
out of which can be squeezed
spells. Each word, then, is a shaft,
a jumbled midden, in which most of the bones
are red deer."
Read dear.

I thought of the cul-de-sac,
of the deer a finger, in manganese, had traced, belling
as if into the end one's head had to be against
to see, a few inches above, the deer.

A belling into the end traced deer.
A belling, into the end, traced. Dear.

The punctuation suddenly looked like turds,
the words animals going off into whitesence,
"their leavings help
guide our reading," Paul was stirring
in Clayton's gut
as if to birth—
but that would be an end to this
if Paul emerged from Clayton.
It is better to keep the stirring a churn,
so that the pus, the dead leaves, the crumpled and
thrown out paths, continue to interchange

"keep me above you" Paul interrupted, "hovering, amazed
that at a 45 degree angle below me
you neither completely fall back nor stand.
As long as you can remain here this way
you inhabit the shaft, the vertical
of yourself, equal to
your height. Your penis emerges from the wall of yourself,
tenderly, nosing about in the rock
for a way to say me. Once I was said as bison,
once there was no separation between driving
a lance in my side,
and being in this shaft. The no separation was a maze
which, read for signs,
kept no separation from coming to conclusion,
so that were I to die before the next line
this line would be entire, an adequate

all, a sagittal

alas.

Printed January 1981 in Santa Barbara & Ann Arbor for the Black Sparrow Press by Mackintosh and Young & Edwards Brothers, Inc. Design by Barbara Martin. This edition is published in paper wrappers; there are 250 hardcover copies numbered & signed by the author; & 35 numbered copies have been handbound in boards by Earle Gray each with a colored holograph poem/drawing by Clayton Eshleman.

Photo: Al Vandenberg

CLAYTON ESHLEMAN was born June 1, 1935, in Indianapolis, Indiana. He was educated at Indiana University and has traveled widely, living in Japan, Korea, Mexico, Peru, and France. In 1979 he shared the National Book Award, with José Rubia Barcia, for *César Vallejo: The Complete Posthumous Poetry* (University of California Press, 1978). He has been the recipient of a Guggenheim Fellowship in Poetry, a National Endowment for the Arts Poetry Fellowship, and a National Endowment for the Humanities "Summer Stipend" Fellowship to support his ongoing research on paleolithic imagination and the construction of the underworld. He is currently teaching creative reading and writing at the California Institute of Technology in Pasadena and, with Annette Smith, translating the complete poetry of Aimé Césaire.